HARRIET BEECHER STOWE

UNCLE TOM's CABIN

Retold: Brett Thomas
Illustrations: Lilian Brøgger
Series editor: Paulette Møller

EASY CLASSICS

Editorial assistance:
Ulla Malmmose, Aschehoug

Cover layout: Jannie Andersen
Cover illustration: Lilian Brøgger

ISBN Denmark: 87-11-09052-9

Printed in Denmark by
Sangill Grafisk Produktion, Holme Olstrup

Harriet Beecher Stowe
(1811-1896)

Harriet Beecher Stowe was born in Connecticut, the youngest member of a family of six brothers and four sisters. Her father was a famous preacher and her brothers and sisters shared an interest in religion. The America that Stowe grew up in was very different from the country we know today. There were many divisions between the North and the South, the most important being the issue of slavery. Many in the North accepted the slavery in the South as necessary for the national economy, although they knew how unfair and immoral this was. Men held all the power and women were expected to be religious and obedient. Until *Uncle Tom's Cabin* first appeared in a Washington newspaper, Stowe's writings were mostly small articles and stories. She was inspired to write her first novel by the stories of cruelty she had heard and read, and by the introduction of the Fugitive Slave Law which obliged the northern states to send runaway slaves back to the South. When *Uncle Tom's Cabin* was finally published in book form it was an instant success, and became the best-seller of the nineteenth century. It was read by politicians, too, and President Lincoln even said that Stowe's writing was one of the causes of the American Civil War (1861-65). It was widely criticized by many people for different reasons: by those in favour of slavery; by some who were against slavery but thought that Stowe's black characters were too simple and docile; by people who did not like her use of black people's dialect; and by others who felt this kind of writing was not acceptable from an American lady. Stowe's later books include *Dred* (1856), *The Minister's Wooing* (1859), *The Pearl of Orr's Island* (1862) and *Oldtown Folks* (1869).
Harriet Beecher Stowe died in 1896.

A Man of Humanity

It was late afternoon on a cold day in February. In a small Kentucky town, two men were sitting and drinking wine. They were talking about a very important subject. One of these men was wearing brightly-coloured clothes, gold rings and a gold watch. He was a slave trader. The other man, Mr Shelby, was quite different. His clothes were elegant and of a good quality. Unlike the trader, he spoke clearly and simply.

"I feel bad about Tom going," said Shelby. "He's hard-working, reliable, honest and manages my farm with no problems..."

"Honest for a *nigger*, you mean!" the trader interrupted.

"No, Haley, I mean honest. Tom is a religious man and I have always trusted him with everything - house, money, horses, everything. One day I asked him to go to *Cincinnati* for me and bring back five hundred dollars from a business up there and he came back with the money, just as I knew he would."

"It's true, there are some Christian niggers around. I got six hundred for one once down in *Orleans*," said the trader.

"Well, Tom's a good man, Haley, and you should take him in exchange for the money I owe you. I'll be sad to see him go."

"As you know, I'm a reasonable man," said the trad-

nigger, an offensive word for a black person
Cincinnati, large town in Ohio, a free state. Tom could have escaped but didn't
Orleans, short form of New Orleans or Nouvelle Orléans, the centre of the slavetrade

er, pouring himself a large glass of brandy, "but that's not a good price, even between friends. Isn't there some little boy or girl you could throw in with Tom?"

At that moment, the door opened and a little boy with light brown skin walked in. He was very handsome and had big, dark eyes and shiny, curly black hair.

"Hey, *Jim Crow*!" said Mr Shelby." Show this gentleman how you dance and sing." The boy began to sing one of the songs that were very popular with black people at the time, and moved his hands and feet in time with his singing.

"Well done!" said Haley, throwing him a piece of orange. Then Mr Shelby told the boy to show how old Elder Robbins sang a *hymn*. The boy made a long, serious face and began to sing slowly through his nose.

"Hurrah!" said Haley. "He's amazing. I have an idea." At this point he put his hand on Mr Shelby's shoulder and looked him in the eye. "Why don't you give me this little one together with Tom and then we have a *deal*."

Again the door opened. This time a beautiful young light-skinned woman came in and picked up the little boy. It was easy to see that this was his mother.

"What is it, Eliza?" asked Mr Shelby.

"Sir, I was just looking for little Harry, please, sir," replied the woman.

"Well, take him with you then, girl," said her master. The mother took the child and quickly closed the door behind her.

Jim Crow, (offensive), an old-fashioned word used to talk about black people
hymn, a religious song
deal, a business agreement

"Wow, she's a beauty!" said Haley. "You could get a good price for her down in Orleans. What are you asking?"

"She's not for sale. My wife will never let her go."

"Fine. So I'll just take the boy, then."

"What would you do with a small boy?" said Shelby.

"They pay well for boys like this one. They train them to work as waiters in *fancy* hotels and restaurants. This one will get a good price."

"I couldn't," said Shelby, thoughtfully, "I'm a *humane* man and I could never take a child away from its mother."

"Well, I'm humane, too, sir. I hate hearing women crying and screaming. But business is business. Now all you have to do is send the girl away for a week or so. You could tell your wife to buy the girl some new earrings or something. She'll soon forget."

"I can't do that!" said Shelby.

"Look, sir, we aren't talking about white people here. These people don't worry about such things. I don't believe in treating women badly like some other people in this business. It makes the girls look ugly and then you don't get a good price for them. It makes my blood run cold when I see how some fellows treat these girls. You have to know how to manage people. Now, I'm not the kind of person who likes to talk about himself, but I must be one of the best in the business. I get some of the finest niggers around and I don't lose many of them. That's because I'm a good manager and because of my humanity. That's what people have told me,

fancy, expensive and elegant
humane, kind-hearted and sympathetic

maybe a hundred times. Yes, sir."

Shelby looked at the trader in silence.

"Now, I know some people don't always agree with me," the trader continued, "but they work fine for me, if I may say so." He laughed.

Shelby laughed, too, but not for the same reason. The trader was happy to have such a good listener. "Now, if I were you, I'd just get the girl out of the way. These niggers *ain't* like us. They don't expect to keep their women or children, or have a good life. Not if you treat them in the right way. But you people up here in Kentucky are too kind to them. So when they go out in the world and get knocked around they ain't ready for it. Now if some of your niggers worked on one of our southern *plantations*, they would all be lonely and depressed. I get my niggers ready for the real world and I would say I treat them as well as they deserve to be treated."

Mr Shelby shook his head. "Now, listen, I'll have to talk this over with my wife, but I don't want you coming around here making my boys nervous. Come and see me this evening and I'll give you you my answer."

The trader put his coat on and left. As he closed the door, Shelby would have liked to kick him down the steps. He didn't know how to tell his wife that he was going to sell Tom to a trader from down south. And what about the boy? His wife would be very angry. He knew that it was his fault. He had bought land that he couldn't pay for and now he needed money.

ain't, 'aren't', in substandard English
plantation, a large farm

Slaves in Kentucky had a better life than slaves in other states. The farm work was not as hard as further south and the masters treated them more kindly. But slaves were not free men. They could be sold by a kind master to an unkind one as soon as there were money problems. In the eyes of the law they were not people, they were things.

Before Eliza opened the door, she had heard the southern trader talking about buying the boy and she was now very upset. Her mistress could see that she was unhappy and asked what was wrong.

"Oh, *missis*!" Eliza cried, with tears in her big, brown eyes. "Please don't let them sell my little Harry."

"What are you talking about, you silly girl!" said Mrs Shelby.

"The trader talking to the master. He said he wanted to buy Harry," said Eliza between her tears.

"Now where do you get these silly ideas, child?" asked Mrs Shelby. "Who in the world would want to take away your baby? Do you think everybody wants to steal your son from you? Now, come here and help me put on this dress, and stop listening at doors. I'd never let anybody take your Harry from you."

Eliza felt a lot better now and began to smile. Mrs Shelby had close contact with the slaves. She had a strong, religious character and her husband left her in charge of the slaves' comfort and education. He was not so strong-minded, and this was why he was worried about his conversation with the trader.

Mrs Shelby knew nothing of her husband's money

missis, Mrs Shelby. Missis was used to talk to the mistress or somebody that was respected

problems and never imagined that he would sell any of their slaves.

Eliza and George

Eliza had grown up in the Shelby house and was admired by local people for her pretty face and good manners. She was married to a young *mulatto* slave called George Harris, from another farm in the area. George's owner hired him out to a local cotton factory where he very soon showed how intelligent he was. After a very short time at the factory he invented a machine that made it easier to clean cotton. George was very popular with the other workers and with the factory manager. George's owner was not so happy. He was a cruel and hard slave-owner, and intelligent slaves made him feel uncomfortable.

He decided to go the factory to take his slave back to the farm. The factory manager could not understand why the slave owner wanted to take George back, and tried to make him change his mind. But the slave owner had already decided George's future.

"But Mr Harris," said the factory owner, "George must stay. I'll give you more money to keep him here. Look at that machine he invented. Please let him stay!"

"That machine!" said the slave owner. "Typical of niggers to think of a way to make work easier! No, I'm taking him back to do some real work on the farm. He's my slave and this is a free country, remember."

So George left the factory with his owner. As he left,

mulatto, half white, half black

the factory owner promised he would try and get George back. The slave could not understand why, after all his good work, he was now being forced to return to the farm.

During his time at the factory George had been given some free time and had been able to see Eliza more often. They married and Eliza had three children. Unfortunately the first two died when they were still small babies. When Harry was born, Eliza was at last able to enjoy the peace and happiness of motherhood.

George began to work on the farm. It became clear that he would never return to the good times at the factory. He grew more and more unhappy. His master gave him the worst and most boring jobs on the farm and he had less and less time to see his wife and son.

While Mrs Shelby was away on her visit, George came to the Shelby house to visit Eliza. Her face lit up and her eyes shone when she saw him. But George did not look so happy.

"Why are you so sad, George?" she asked. "See how happy I am and how fine your son looks."

"I wish I'd never seen him and I wish you'd never met me," said George with an angry look in his eyes. Eliza began to cry. "Oh, George, why are you so sad?" she asked, with tears rolling down her pretty face.

"I've had enough. I work every hour of the day as hard as I can and what do I get? - kicks, punches and insults. Last week *Mas'r* told me he didn't want no nigger dogs on his farm and he told me to throw little Carlo in the river with a stone around its neck."

Mas'r, the master, slave-owner

"You didn't do it!" cried Eliza.

"Of course not, my love. Mas'r and his son killed it and then *whipped* me for not doing it myself. One of these days I'm going to teach them a lesson."

"Oh, George! Don't do anything silly. Believe in God and He will take care of you."

"Eliza, you know I'm not a Christian. I can't believe in God when life is so terrible. You haven't heard the worst yet."

"What has happened, George to make you so angry?"

"Well, you know my master hates Shelby and his

whip, to hit someone with a stick

friends. Now he says he doesn't want me coming over here. He wants me to marry Mina and stay at his place. If not, he'll sell me down *the river*."

"He can't do that. You're married to me. We had a proper Christian wedding, just like white people," cried Eliza.

"Oh, wife, you must know that a slave can't marry. There's no law for that in this country. That's why I wish you'd never met me and that we'd never had our son. If my master wants to separate us, there's nothing to stop him. And what kind of life will there be for little Harry?"

"But the Shelbys are so kind and good to us, George," said Eliza.

"Yes, but you never know what can happen. If one day they need money, they can get good money for a handsome and intelligent boy."

Eliza remembered the conversation between the southern trader and Mr Shelby earlier that day and was suddenly afraid. She was just about to tell him but then decided it would only make her husband more unhappy.

"So, Eliza, my love," said George with tears in his eyes. "You must look after yourself and our son. Tonight I'm leaving you."

"Leaving? Where are you going, George?" asked Eliza nervously.

"To Canada and freedom. I'll make money and come back to buy your freedom. I'll die before I let them sell

the river, here, the Mississippi River. Selling a slave down the river meant sending him or her to the Deep South where life was even harder for slaves.

me down south. So *pray* for me, Eliza. Perhaps your God will look after me."

For a few minutes they stood there in silence, holding hands and crying quietly. Then George was gone and the family was separated.

Uncle Tom

Uncle Tom's cabin was a small building made of wooden *logs*, and was very close to his master's house. Around the house there were gardens which in summer were full of strawberries, raspberries and other fruit. There were also all kinds of different flowers including a big climbing rose plant that grew all over the wooden sides of the cabin.

Inside, Aunt Chloe was making supper for her husband after having made the evening meal at the Shelby house where she was head cook. Her black, round and smiling face shone with *satisfaction* as she took one of her famous cakes out of the oven. In one corner of the small cabin there was a bed and, in another corner, two curly-haired boys were trying to teach their little sister to walk. All three of them smiled each time the little one managed to take two steps forward before falling on her bottom.

In front of the fire was an old wooden table covered with pretty plates and cups. A meal was about to be put on the table, and a big strong black man with a serious face and a quiet manner was sitting on a chair. Uncle

pray, to talk to God
logs, round pieces of wood, from cut-down trees
satisfaction, happiness, contentment

Tom was writing some letters on a *slate*, helped by a thirteen-year-old white boy. This was Mas'r George, Shelby's son, who was teaching Uncle Tom to write.

"No, Tom, that's not a 'g', that's a 'q'. The line goes the other way, look."

"Oh, that's right, Mas'r George. I'll try it again," said the big man, slowly moving the pencil over the slate with his big, heavy fingers.

"I'm *awfully* hungry, Aunt Chloe," said the young teacher. "They wanted me to have supper in the house, but I didn't want to miss your cakes."

"Well, you just sit down there with my Tom, young man. Come on, you two, Mose and Pete," she said, pushing her sons away to a corner, "you run along while I get some sausages on the table."

Mas'r George and Tom quickly finished off another delicious meal while Aunt Chloe fed her little baby.

"Those boys almost *drive* me *crazy* with all their laughing and shouting. I don't know what I'm going to do with them, I really don't," she said with a stern look on her face. "Now come on and go to bed. We're going to have our meeting."

"Oh, Mum, we want to stay for the meeting. We like them. Please let us stay, please," said the boys pulling their mother's dress.

"Let them stay, Aunt Chloe," said young Mas'r George.

"Well, all right, maybe it will do them some good," said the big black woman, smiling.

Very soon the small cabin was crowded with other

slate, a flat, grey stone which people used to write on
awfully, here, very or really
drive me crazy, make me mad

slaves of all ages. From an old man of eighty years to a fifteen-year-old girl. Not all of them were from the Shelby farm. Some came from other houses in the area. After a lot of friendly introductions, the "meeting" started. They all sang hymns, some of them from the local churches and others they had picked up at camp meetings. Many of the hymns were about a happy future and the "promised land" and the singers *clapped* and held hands as they sang.

Then an old lady stood up and talked about how she was getting ready to go to the land of glory and what a beautiful day that would be. Mas'r George was asked to read the last chapters of the Book of Revelations from the Bible.

Uncle Tom was greatly respected by the others and was rather like a *minister* for them. In very simple language he led the others in *prayers*, which were often interrupted by a shout or cheer from one of the others.

While all this was happening, Shelby and Haley, the southern slave-trader, were counting money on the dining-room table in the house.

"Yes, that's just right," said the trader. "Now, if you'll sign these papers, everything will be done."

"Before I sign, Haley," said Shelby, looking him in the eye, "I want you to promise me that you'll never sell Tom to anybody who'll not treat him well."

"Well, of course," replied the trader. "You have my word that I'll do the best I can. There's nothing in the

clap, hit the hands together to make a noise
minister, religious leader
prayer, the words you say to God

world I hate more than cruelty."

When Haley had gone, Shelby sat quietly in a chair smoking a cigar. He felt very unsure of Haley's promise, but knew that there was nothing more he could do.

Decision Time

While Mrs Shelby brushed her hair before going to bed, her husband sat in a chair in the bedroom, quietly watching her in the mirror. Eliza usually helped her, but Mrs Shelby had told her she could go to bed early tonight as she was looking a little pale and tired.

"Oh, yes. Who was that horrible man you were talking to this morning?"

"His name's Haley," her husband replied. "I met him on business once down in Natchez."

"Why did he come so far for dinner?"

"I invited him up here. We had some business to talk about."

"Is he a slave trader?" asked Mrs Shelby, seeing that her husband looked a little nervous.

"What makes you think that?"

"Eliza told me she heard you talking about selling her boy. She was very upset, crying all the time. I told her we would never do that, especially to a man like Haley."

"Emily," said Shelby, standing next to his wife. "I always said that too but times are hard."

"What do you mean?" she asked, turning to face her husband.

"I have business problems and I'm afraid I have to sell some of my servants," he answered. "I've sold Tom."

"Tom? Our good, faithful Tom! You promised him

his freedom only the other day. Well, I can believe anything now! Why, I even believe you could sell Eliza's little boy, her only child!"

"I'm afraid you're right," said Shelby looking away. "I've sold them both - Harry and Tom. And I don't know why you are shouting at me for doing what everybody else does."

"But why those two slaves when you have so many others," asked his wife.

"Because I can get the best price for them," replied Shelby. "You should be glad. He wanted to buy Eliza, too."

"This is terrible," said Mrs Shelby, trying to control her anger. "How will I ever be able to face our people again after all my talk of Christian values and the importance of the family. This slavery is such an awful thing. I have always hated our laws which allow us to treat people like objects to buy and sell. How stupid I was to think that I could give our people better lives here than if they were free."

"Well, the minister at the church has a better opinion of slavery and he's a Christian," said Shelby.

"Well, don't think you'll see me in that church again! A man of the church defending such evil is something I will never understand."

After a short silence, Mrs Shelby asked her husband if they could sell her gold watch and buy the little boy back from Haley. But it was too late. The papers were signed, the slaves were now the property of the trader. Next morning Haley was to take his new possessions south with him. Shelby thought that it would be a good idea if his wife went for a walk with Eliza so that the little boy could be taken away quietly.

"Never!" said Mrs Shelby. "I have no intention of helping anybody in this."

Outside the room somebody was listening to every word with wide-open eyes and her heart beating wildly. Eliza's normally soft and gentle looks were much harder now as she hurried back to her cabin. She took everything she could carry, as well as some of little Harry's favourite toys and put them in a bag. She picked him up and dressed him, still half asleep, before running out into the cold dark night. She ran past the Shelby house and over to Uncle Tom's cabin. There she told Aunt Chloe and Tom everything she had heard at the house. As Tom heard the terrible news, he sank slowly down into his chair and covered his face with his hands.

"Well, old man," said Chloe looking at Tom. "Why don't you go, too? You don't want to be sold down the river where you'll die of hard work and hunger. Go with Eliza. I'll get your things together for you."

But Tom just stood up and walked over to the corner where his curly-haired sons were sleeping. Big tears began to roll down his strong black face.

"I can't go. Mas'r didn't want to sell me, Chloe. I've always stood by him and I know he's doing what he thinks is best. I'm not going to run away. Let Eliza go with her boy."

Eliza asked Tom and Chloe to get word to her husband that she was running away to Canada and freedom. Then she ran out of the cabin door and away into the darkness.

Discovery

It was later than usual when Shelby and his wife woke the next day. When Andy, one of the boys in the house, told them of Eliza's escape, their first reaction was surprise. Then Mrs Shelby was happy and her husband was angry. There was a lot of noise and people ran all over the place, banging doors and shouting. Only Aunt Chloe stayed quiet, baking her biscuits as if she knew nothing of Eliza and Harry.

Later, when Haley arrived, all the farm hands smiled broadly as they told the slave-trader the news and heard his vulgar reaction. Their laughter only made Haley even more angry and when he walked into the house, he could hardly hide his *rage*.

"What's this I hear, Shelby, about you letting the girl run away? We had a deal!" he shouted.

It took a long time before Shelby was able to get Haley to sit down and try to relax. They agreed to have breakfast while Shelby's slaves got some horses ready. Mrs Shelby stayed away from the breakfast table, not wanting to talk to the southern trader. Outside, the confusion continued. People were talking about what was going to happen to old Tom and where Eliza could be. No work was done and everything was a lot slower than usual. The servants took a long time to make and serve breakfast and Haley grew more and more nervous. Only two or three cups of fresh coffee seemed to help.

After breakfast, Haley walked outside to get on his white horse and ride after Eliza, but the stable boys had other ideas. One of them, Sam, had put a beech nut

rage, anger

under the *saddle* of Haley's horse. At first the horse didn't notice it. But when Haley who was a big, heavy man, swung himself into the saddle, the horse went wild with pain, standing on its back legs and sending Haley crashing to the ground before running off as fast as its legs could carry it. Mrs Shelby had a good idea of what Sam had done and smiled down from her bedroom window at Haley's rage and the amusement of the onlookers. It was twelve o'clock before Sam and the boys finally brought Haley's horse back to the house. They made sure that the horse was very hot and tired before they returned, though.

"That's three hours I've lost with these horses," said Haley. "Now, come on, let's move. We need to get that nigger girl back."

"We can't do that, Mas'r!" said Sam, pointing at the horses. "Look how tired the horses are. I'm sure Missis doesn't want us to hurt the horses. Maybe we should wait until after lunch."

At this point, Mrs Shelby suddenly became very friendly and told Haley he should stay for lunch, promising that it would be on the table very quickly. As the unhappy slave-trader walked back into the house, Mrs Shelby looked around. Sam and his friend saw her smile and they smiled back before taking the horses for a good, long wash.

Eliza's Escape

Eliza ran and ran, through the darkness and past the farmhouses she knew in the area. She carried little Har-

saddle, the seat used on a horse

ry in her arms, never stopping to think how heavy he was. Every time she felt tired she thought of the slave-trader taking away her only son and this gave her new strength. In the early morning she came to an area she had never seen before. She was afraid that people riding by would ask why she was running and where she was going, so she let little Harry walk sometimes. As her skin was very light, people didn't stop and ask questions.

On and on she walked, never stopping to eat. Harry had eaten all the apples and cakes she had taken with her. The need to escape was so powerful that she didn't feel hungry. She kept Harry quiet by telling him that they were running away from a very bad man who

wanted to take him away from her. The sun was setting when she reached a small town on the banks of the Ohio River, separating the states of Ohio and Kentucky. The river was the first stage on her escape to freedom, so we can imagine how she felt when she saw that the river was full of floating ice that came down from the mountains in early springtime. No boat would cross the river in those conditions.

She turned away from the river and walked into a small *tavern* where a woman prepared the evening meal.

"Is there no boat across today?" Eliza asked.

"Not with all this ice," said the woman. "You seem to be in a hurry to cross."

"I have a sick child across the river," said Eliza. "I've walked all day to get the boat."

The woman's husband said, "If you wait until after supper, there's a man called Sol who said he was going to try and cross tonight."

After his long and tiring day on the road, little Harry began to cry. The woman took him into a small side-room where he quickly fell asleep. Eliza stayed with him, holding his little hands, and watching from the window the big blocks of ice floating down the river.

Back at the house, Mrs Shelby's promise of a quick lunch for Haley was not being kept. There seemed to be lots of problems, getting messages from Mrs Shelby to Aunt Chloe, and from Aunt Chloe to the other servants who were helping her. Everyone could see that Mrs Shelby was not too worried about this, and they

tavern, a place where you can buy food and drink

did their best to make as many mistakes and have as many accidents as was possible in a kitchen.

"Let him wait," said Aunt Chloe holding a fork in her hand. "He deserves it. God will find him and send him to Hell, just like Tom tells us from the Bible."

"And he'll burn forever, too," said young Andy.

"You don't know what you're saying," said a voice that made them all turn and look to the door. It was Tom who was listening to their conversation. "We should pray for them - the ones that use you badly. That's what the Bible says."

"Pray for them that take a baby from his mother and sell him? Them that dress in their nice clothes and spend all their money on drinking and smoking? It's too hard, I can't pray for those people," said Aunt Chloe and began to cry into her cooking apron.

Then Tom was called to the house to speak to Mr Shelby.

"Tom," he said, "you know this man is going to take you with him tomorrow. But today you can do what you want. You are free for the rest of the day."

"But I don't want any of your dirty nigger tricks!" shouted Haley.

"Mas'r," said Tom."Have I ever done anything bad to you or lied to you?"

"No you haven't Tom, that's the truth. And I would do anything in the world not to have to sell you."

"And as sure as I am a Christian," said Mrs Shelby, "I want you to tell me where Tom goes. When I get the money I'll buy him back."

"Well, that sounds good to me," said Haley. "That's how I make my money, buying and selling. We all have to make money somehow."

For the next two hours, Mrs Shelby tried to say as little as possible to the trader, hoping that Eliza was far, far away. When Haley left he took Andy and Sam with him. There were two possible roads to the river, one which was straight and used by horses and carriages and another, older road which almost nobody used. After a lot of discussion Haley decided that Eliza must have taken the old road, so they all rode their horses over stones and dust until they had to stop. The road was closed and a big farmhouse stood at the end of it. Haley was very angry. They had to ride back to the other road, which meant they lost another hour. They arrived at the river not long after little Harry had fallen asleep.

As soon as Eliza saw the three men riding past the window, she picked up Harry and ran as fast as she could down to the side of the river. Haley saw her running in the distance and rode after her, Andy and Sam coming more slowly behind.

Eliza didn't have time to think. For one second she stopped at the side of the river, saw Haley coming closer and jumped onto a big piece of floating ice. She couldn't feel her feet as she jumped from one piece of ice to another over the cold water until, with one big jump, she came to the other side. As if in a dream she tried to climb with Harry up over the grassy river bank. Then a hand, the hand of a farmer who lived near the Shelbys, pulled her up onto the top of the bank.

"Why, it's Shelby's girl. What are you doing up here?" he asked her.

Gasping for breath, she pointed a finger to the Kentucky side of the river and said, "That man. He wants to sell my little Harry. Mr Symmes, you have a little boy yourself!"

"That's right. You're a brave girl and I like to see it, Eliza. But I don't know where to take you. Why don't you try that house over there?" said Symmes, pointing to a very big house about two miles away. "They're good people. They'll help you."

Symmes was not an expert in his country's laws and didn't know that it was against the law to help runaway slaves. If he had known better, it would have been harder for him to do it.

On the other side of the river, Haley could not believe what he had seen.

"That girl jumped like a wild cat!" he said.

"Don't ask us to follow her across, Mas'r," said Sam, laughing. "I don't think my feet are fast enough for that."

As Sam and Andy began to cry with laughter, Haley took his whip and began to swing it at them. The two slaves jumped on their horses at the top of the river bank and rode back to the Shelby house, leaving Haley by the river.

Haley went back to the tavern to decide what was to be done. He had a few glasses of whisky to help him think. After his third or fourth glass, he saw two men getting off their horses outside. He looked a little closer and saw that one of them was Tom Loker, somebody he had done business with once or twice down south. Loker was a big, hard-looking man with a dirty, black beard and cruel eyes. Marks, the other man, was very different. He was small, thin and nervous with sharp eyes and a *crooked* smile that showed his few remaining

crooked, not straight

teeth to be yellow and brown.

Haley now believed his luck was changing. Tom Loker hated black people and was just the person Haley needed to bring back a runaway slave and her baby. Loker was no friend of Haley's but business was business, so the trader took out some money and told the man behind the bar to keep filling the whisky glasses. After some time, Haley began to tell the story of Eliza's escape and about the boy he had paid for.

"Running all over the country after a nigger woman, eh?" said Marks with a nervous smile.

"I never have such problems," said Loker, drying his mouth with the sleeve of his dirty shirt. "I just hold my hand up to their face and say, 'Now listen, if you give me any trouble I'll smash your face.' And I tell them the baby's mine and I'm going to sell it. If they start crying or making trouble..." and he struck the table with his heavy hand. Marks began to laugh as he watched Haley's face.

"Now, if I understand you right, Mr Haley," said Marks, "you want us to bring in the girl for you."

"You can do what you want with the girl. She's Shelby's problem. I just want that boy," said Haley.

"And what does this girl look like?"

"She's got very light skin, very fine-looking and educated," Haley explained. "I was going to give Shelby a thousand dollars for her."

"Well, well, I think we could make a deal here," said Marks, his eyes shining. "How does this sound? We bring the boy back for you, take the girl for ourselves and sell her in Orleans."

Now Haley had found someone to catch his "property" and bring him back. After many more whiskies and in the middle of the night, Marks and Tom Loker took the same boat that Eliza had been waiting for to carry her across the icy river.

A Politician with Human Feelings

Senator Bird sat down in a comfortable armchair in front of the fire and took off his boots. His wife was looking happy as she took charge of the tea table.

"Well, this is a nice surprise," she said after some time. "We didn't know you were coming home tonight."

"Well, I needed to come back and have some rest. All this travelling around the state talking to people makes a man tired. What I need is a cup of your good tea and a quiet evening at home. Making laws is a tough job."

"And what new laws have you been making in the *Senate*? What they say can't be true, that you are going to stop people giving food and drink to runaway slaves, can it? It doesn't seem at all Christian," asked Mrs Bird.

"Well, yes, it's true that we are trying to stop slaves coming here from Kentucky. The farmers in Kentucky are not too happy and we must try and be good neighbours."

"So does the law now say that we are not allowed to give people who are hungry, tired and cold something to make their life a little better and help them on their way?"

Senator, a member of the Senate in Washington, D.C., the capital of the United States
Senate, a place where elected politicians - senators - meet (in Washington)

Mrs Bird was a very quiet little lady who very rarely lost control of her feelings. But she hated cruelty. This was too much for her. She stood up and looked her husband in the eye.

"Now, John, tell me this. Do you think that kind of law is Christian?"

"Mary, listen. You shouldn't let your heart rule your head. *Governing* a country means that you have to think about other people's interests and not let your own colour your judgement."

"I know nothing about politics. But I know that the Bible says we must help those in need."

"But Mary, sometimes we do wrong by helping others and..."

"Good can never hurt other people!" interrupted Mrs Bird.

The Senator was not a cold-hearted man and he found this kind of discussion difficult. He was much happier cleaning his reading-glasses and coughing. But Mrs Bird had not finished.

"Would you send a woman away if she came to our house in a snow-storm, or put her in prison, John Bird?"

"Well, the law says..." he started to say.

"The law! You politicians always find ways of turning things around. You can't see the difference between simple right and wrong. But I know you, John, and you would never send anyone to prison who was dying of hunger."

At this moment, one of the servants came in and

gorvern, to control, to rule

said there was a girl outside with a baby. The Senator sat down happily in his chair again, next to the fire. But only for a second.

"John! John! Quickly! Come to the kitchen!" his wife called.

Eliza was lying on the kitchen floor. She had only one shoe, and her torn stockings were covered in blood. Her clothes were torn and frozen with the cold.

"She just came into the warm kitchen here and fell on the floor!" said one of the black servants. "A pretty woman, too. Look at those hands, she's never worked in the fields."

They rubbed Eliza and little Harry's hands and feet to try and wake them.

"Oh, Harry! Where's Harry? Have they got him?" she asked as soon as she opened her eyes.

Hearing his mother's cry, Harry woke, too, and ran to her.

"Please don't let them take my boy! Please, Missis, please!" she cried, looking at Mrs Bird.

A bed was prepared near the fire and Eliza fell asleep, holding Harry close to her as she slept. Mr and Mrs Bird said nothing for a while. Mrs Bird started *knitting* as her husband looked at the newspaper without really reading it.

Then Mr Bird put down his paper and said, "I know that she's much taller than you, Mary, but haven't you got a dress she could wear?"

His wife smiled as she said, "I'll go and look."

"And that old coat you never wear. She could have that, too," said the Senator.

knit, to make clothes with wool and long needles

Some hours later Eliza woke and told them the story of her crossing the river and escaping.

"But the river's full of ice!" said one of the servants.

"I know. But I just ran and jumped and God helped me across. I don't know how I did it," Eliza explained.

"But was your master cruel to you?" asked the Senator.

"Oh, no. He was very kind but..." and Eliza saw that Mrs Bird was wearing black clothes. "Have you ever lost a child, Missis?"

Mrs Bird had lost her youngest child only one month before. Mr Bird held his wife's hands as tears came to her gentle eyes.

"Yes, yes. I've lost a little one."

"Well, you'll understand me, Missis. I've lost two and he's the only one I have now. But they wanted to take him, so I ran away. I'll die before I let them take him from me. They wanted to sell him, so I ran across the ice and then a man helped me up the river bank."

"And where do you plan to go now," asked the Senator, trying to control his feelings.

"Canada," answered Eliza.

"Canada? Do you know how far that is from here?" he asked.

"It's a very long way, my poor girl," said Mrs Bird. "But tonight you must stay here. I'll make a bed for you and we'll think what to do in the morning. But don't worry, my child. God will look after you."

Shortly after Eliza had left the room with her tired son, the Senator began to think again. He knew how hard it was to hide a woman with a young child from somebody like Haley. He was also worried about his political position. What would people say about a Senator giving help to a runaway slave? But Mrs Bird could see that her husband had a plan.

Putting on his boots he told her, "They can't stay here. I'll take them away to a place where they'll be safe. An old friend, Van Trompe, freed all his slaves and bought a place in the woods. It's a difficult road so I'll take them myself. When I've left them, I'll go on up to Columbus, where I can start work early tomorrow morning."

So Mrs Bird woke up the mother and child and, after filling a big suitcase with clothes said goodbye to them. Mr Bird helped them into his carriage and sat at the front with his servant, Cudjoe. The road was terrible. The heavy rain of the last two months had left big holes and the Senator needed all his experience of the road to drive slowly up into the woods and hills. Eliza and Harry were thrown up and down in the back of the carriage as it turned sharp corners and crossed fast-moving, icy rivers. It was after midnight when the carriage finally stopped in front of a very dark and quiet farmhouse.

After some minutes the owner opened the door to the visitors. John Van Trompe was a big man with a big heart. He had come to Ohio from Kentucky, where he owned a big farm. After years of seeing what a hard life the slaves had, he bought some land in Ohio, gave all his slaves letters of freedom and let them live and work as free people on the new land. Then he had bought this little farm in the hills where he could live a very quiet, peaceful life.

"Are you the man to protect a mother and child from slave-catchers?" the Senator asked the big man.

"I am," said Van Trompe. "And I have six big sons

who are ready to help me." He took a close look at Eliza. "You're a pretty woman, that's for sure. But it's often the pretty ones who have to run, in my experience. Now you just come through into this little bedroom with your boy. You can sleep as long as you like. Nobody will give you any trouble while I'm here."

The Senator told his friend what he knew about Eliza's escape from Kentucky and about the slave-trader Haley.

"It's a terrible thing. I tell you, I was so tired of hearing churchmen defending slavery and trading, I began to speak against them. Then I found a minister who read the Bible the way I understood it and spoke out against such things. That's when I joined the church."

Some minutes later Senator Bird and old Cudjoe were back in the carriage, riding on towards Columbus, the capital of Ohio.

Tom's Last Morning

Tom was sitting inside his cabin, his Bible on his knee, as the rain beat on the windows on this cold February morning. Aunt Chloe stood in front of the fire, ironing all Tom's shirts and every now and then wiping tears from her face with her apron. The children were still sleeping in their little bed in the corner. Tom stood up and walked over to Chloe.

"It's the last time," he said.

"There's nothing we can do," said Chloe. "Missis said she'd buy you back in one or two years. But I've heard that a man can die down south in less than a year. Nobody ever comes back."

"They have the same God there as we do here and I thank Him that He chose to send me down there and not you or the children," he said.

"I don't understand how God can let such horrible things happen," said Chloe, with tears rolling down over her face.

"I'm in His hands and He'll look after me," said Tom, trying to be strong.

The family sat down to their last breakfast together. Tom was not very hungry and looked from one face to another as they ate their chicken and bread. Aunt Chloe didn't seem to be enjoying her chicken. She cried and cried as she thought about the day when her sons, too, would be sold down south. Mrs Shelby ran through the rain and entered the cabin as they were finishing their breakfast.

"Tom," she said, looking at Chloe's wet, pale face. "I just wanted to say..." But she couldn't get the words out. She, too, began to cry. Soon everybody in the cabin was drying their eyes.

"I promise before God," said Mrs Shelby, "that I'll do everything I can to buy you and bring you back here. You must believe that God will look after you until then."

At that moment they saw Haley walking towards the cabin.

"Come on, nigger!" he shouted as he kicked the door open. "Are you ready?"

Then he saw Mrs Shelby sitting there with Tom's family.

"Oh! Good morning Ma'am," he said, taking his hat off.

Tom picked up his suitcase, leaving the cabin and his

family behind him and walked over to the horse and carriage, where the other slaves and servants were gathered.

"Get in!" said Haley, pushing Tom into the seat of the carriage and taking some chains which he put around Tom's feet and hands.

"Mr Haley," said Mrs Shelby with a very angry face.

"There is no need to chain Tom. He'd never run away."

"I've already lost five hundred dollars from this house and I'll decide what to do with my own property," said Haley and took his place in the carriage.

"I'm sorry I can't say goodbye to Mas'r George," said Tom looking at Mrs Shelby, whose son was visiting a friend for a few days. Mr Shelby was also away from home. He couldn't bear to stay and see Tom leave. He knew that he had done something that was correct in the eyes of the law of the country but that did not make him feel any better. He had told his wife he had business in the north.

Haley whipped up the horses as fast as they could gallop, slowing down a little once they were out of sight of the house. After an hour's ride along the dusty road Haley stopped, leaving Tom sitting sadly in the carriage. While he sat thinking about the future that awaited him, a pair of young arms were suddenly thrown around his neck. It was Mas'r George, who had heard about his father selling Uncle Tom to the trader.

"Oh, Uncle Tom, Uncle Tom!" he cried. "How could they have done this? If I was a man, they wouldn't have done it. I would have stopped them."

"I'm so glad to see you, Mas'r George. It makes my heart glad just to see you."

"I've brought you my silver dollar, Uncle Tom. And I made a hole in it so this horrible man can't take it away from you." Young George tied the silver dollar around the big man's neck. "And remember, every time you see this dollar, that one day I'll find you and bring you back. I'll show my father what a big mistake he's made."

"Now, George," said Tom putting his hand on

George's shoulder, "don't say anything against your family. They have been good to me and you should be glad. You're a good boy and one day you'll be able to use all your reading and writing so that they're proud of you."

At this point Haley came walking back towards the carriage.

"I hope you feel real bad - buying and selling people and putting chains on them like animals," said George.

"It's your kind with all their money, who do all the buying and selling who should feel bad. They keep people like me alive," answered Haley.

"Days like these make me feel ashamed to be from Kentucky," continued the young boy. "Goodbye, Uncle Tom. We'll meet again." Tom felt the silver dollar hanging warmly against his heart as young George rode off on his horse. He smiled.

The Slave Market

As Haley drove the carriage along the dusty road, he was thinking about the price he was going to get for his slave. Sometimes he was so bored he almost began a conversation with Tom, but then he remembered that people like Tom could only think and talk about freedom. Tom was thinking about different parts of the Bible, which gave him courage and strength now the future looked so unhappy.

Haley pulled some cuttings of newspapers out of his coat pocket and began to read them. Tom could see that the trader was not a good reader.

"There it is," said the white man. "In Washington,

Kentucky on February 20, there'll be a sale of the following Negroes: Hagar, aged 60; John, aged 30; Ben, aged 21; Saul, aged 25; Albert, aged 14. I'm going to have a look at that." He looked over at Tom, who did not seem very interested. "I'm going to buy some people to come along with us so that you'll have somebody to talk to."

Tom thought about these men and women and how many of them had husbands, wives, children or friends that they would never see again. They travelled all day and it was evening before they got to the small town of Washington, Kentucky. Haley found himself a cheap hotel before taking Tom to the *jail*, where he was to sleep for the night.

The next day a crowd of white men stood outside the *court-house*, waiting for the sale to begin. On one side stood the group of slaves. One of them, Hagar, was sixty years old, but a life of hard work and illness made her look many years older. She stood with the only son she had left, Albert. The rest of the family had been sold a long time ago. The white men walked around the slaves, sometimes telling them to open their mouths, and show their teeth, just as if they were buying a horse or a dog. Hagar was afraid her son was going to be separated from her.

"I'm old but I can work as well as anybody. I'm a good cook, too," she told the buyers, who were more interested in her son.

jail, a small prison
court-house, a public building where the officials decide if a person has done something which is against the law

"I think I'll buy the boy," said Haley to another buyer standing next to him.

"They're selling the woman and the boy together," said the other.

"Somebody else can buy her. She's a bag of bones and almost blind."

"It's a pity to take a mother away from her only son. You can see how much she loves the boy."

"That's her problem," said Haley, putting a cigar in his mouth.

At that point, the man who organized the sale pushed the boy away from his mother and out into the middle of the crowd.

"Please, Mas'r. Please sell us together," said the poor woman, trying to bring her son back.

"Be quiet and stay where you are," said the seller as the sale began.

Haley bought two of the men for what he thought was a good price and they were taken to one side. Different people were interested in the boy but it was Haley who bought him in the end. He was pushed towards his new owner but turned around for the last time towards his mother.

"Please, Mas'r, buy me, too, for God's sake. I'll die if you don't!" she cried, holding out her arms to Haley.

"You'll die in any case," said the trader as he turned around and walked away, taking his three new slaves with him. He put them into the carriage, put chains around their arms and legs and then chained them all together with Tom. It was some days before they got to the river and onto a boat. The boat came from Ohio and a flag with the stars and stripes waved overhead. Up on deck, well-dressed people were walking up and

down, enjoying the winter sun and the view from the boat. Below deck, the four slaves sat in the dark, thinking about the loved ones they had left behind. The boat made several stops and after one long stop, Tom saw that Haley was walking onto the boat with a pretty young black girl holding a small baby. She was smiling happily as she sat down on her suitcase.

As the boat pulled away to continue its journey, Haley came back and began to talk to the woman. Tom saw that suddenly the woman's face changed and she did not seem so happy.

"I don't believe it, I can't believe it," Tom heard her say.

"Well, here are the papers," said Haley, pulling documents from his pocket and smiling. "Your master sold you to me for good money. Ask one of these men to read it if you like."

One of the white men began to read the document.

"John Fosdick agrees to sell the girl Lucy and her child to the trader, Mr Haley. That's what it says here."

People began to crowd around them to see what the trouble was.

"But Mas'r said I was going down to *Louisville* to work with my husband as a cook. I can't believe he'd do

Louisville, large town in Kentucky

this!" said the poor woman.

"That's what it says on the paper," said another of the men who were there.

"Well, there's nothing more to say, then," said the girl Lucy, looking back towards the river.

Around her people went on talking but she did not seem to hear. A gentle *breeze* blew through her hair and took the heat of the evening sunshine from her face. Her heart felt like a stone inside her. It was only when her baby touched her face with his little hands that she woke up, looked down at him and began to cry.

breeze, a light wind

"That's a fine young boy," said one of the men, looking at Lucy's ten-month-old son.

"Thank you," said Lucy, as the man took some chocolate out of his pocket and gave it to the boy. Two minutes later the same man was talking to Haley on the other side of the boat.

"Pretty girl," he said, lighting a big cigar. "Are you taking her south?"

"Yes, I guess so," said Haley. "She's got the good fine fingers that cotton-farmers like to see. She's a good cook, too, so I'll sell her somewhere, for sure."

"A cotton-farmer won't buy the boy, though," said the man.

"I'll sell him as soon as I can," said Haley.

"I need a new little one," continued the man. "I lost one last week when one of my servants was doing the washing. Her little boy fell into the water and drowned. I thought she could have this one instead."

In the end the boy was sold for forty-five dollars and both men seemed happy with that.

"Where do you live?" asked Haley.

"Louisville," said his new customer.

"Louisville," continued Haley. "Well, that's all right. The little boy'll be asleep. I'll take him away from his mother then. I don't like all the *row* they make when you take a baby away. I like to do things quietly."

Louisville is where Lucy's husband lived. When the boat began to slow down, she stood up and walked to the side of the boat, hoping to see him there, next to the river. Her little boy was still asleep where she left him. Haley saw all this and told the stranger, "Now's

row, a noisy argument

your chance. Quietly, now. I don't want any crying."

The man walked off the boat taking the baby with him, without Lucy noticing. She was looking for her husband's face in the crowd. Tom saw it all, though, and he could imagine what would happen next. When the boat began to move again, Lucy walked very sadly back to where she had left her sleeping baby. But she only saw Haley.

"Where…?" she started to ask.

"Listen, Lucy," said the trader. "Your boy's gone. You couldn't take the boy with you down south and a good family offered a fine home for him, so I sold him. They'll look after him better than you can."

Haley had seen and done this kind of thing so many times before that he was less interested in the *grief* of a mother losing her only child than in all the noise she could make. He hated slave mothers making a lot of *fuss* about losing their children. This time he was happy. Lucy did not say a word. She simply looked away into the dark night. She saw and heard nothing but just looked into the blackness of the dark night.

Although Haley did not like noise, he did not like such a silent reaction either, so he continued to talk. Talking made **him** feel better, at least.

"Don't worry, Lucy. A fine girl like you will find another husband and I'm sure…"

"Please, Mas'r, don't talk to me, now," said the young woman, turning away from the trader.

Tom watched as Haley got up and walked away. He thought what a cruel thing he had just seen. Tom's

grief, extreme sadness
fuss, a lot of noise and confusion

world was a small one and what he thought was cruel, other people called business. The horror and stupidity of the slave-trade was defended all over America. Even in many of the churches, religious leaders would find small passages in the *Old Testament* which, they said, spoke of the need for buying and selling slaves, and the separation of human beings from those they loved. But Tom was a simple man and his feelings told him that what had happened was wrong. He tried to speak to Lucy, hoping to make her a little happier. He spoke with his soft voice of a heart full of love in the skies, of Jesus and of Heaven, but the girl did not seem to hear.

As it got darker, people went to their beds and Tom, too, lay down to sleep. Lucy sat there waiting for a helping hand to come from the skies. Tom could hear her saying, "Oh, God! What shall I do? Help me, please!" and then there was silence.

In the middle of the night a noise woke Tom up. It was the sound of something falling into the big river. He looked up. The woman was gone. He looked over the side of the boat but could see nothing. The river was as quiet as before and Lucy was lost forever.

Next morning the trader woke early and came down to check his property.

"Where's the nigger-girl?" he said, waking Tom. Tom told him he had heard the noise of something falling off the boat in the middle of the night. The trader was not really surprised. He had seen this kind of thing so often before. He just sat down and thought how unlucky he was. If his journey continued like this he

Old Testament, the first part of the Bible before Jesus Christ was born

was going to make very little money for all his hard work. He asked himself how life could be so hard on a man like him. He was only trying to do a job, after all.

The *Quakers*

Back in Ohio, Eliza was enjoying a quiet and peaceful life among the Quaker community. She had lost some of her bright, girlish prettiness after the difficulties of the last weeks. Now her face was a little more serious and pale. She spent most of her time helping the Quaker women when they cooked, cleaned and *sewed*. Little Harry was always nearby and a minute never passed without her making sure he was there, and safe and sound. The Quaker women with their simple clothes and their friendly rosy faces were always helpful and caring, but Eliza knew what she wanted to do and where she wanted to go.

"Do you still want to go to Canada, then, Eliza?" asked Rachel, one of the Quaker women.

"Yes ma'am, I must," said Eliza with a serious face.

"But what will you do there my child?"

"I don't know ma'am. But I must go. I'll do whatever I can. There's always something."

A little later, a big strong man, Simeon Holliday, walked into the house. His wife, Ruth, was sitting sewing with Rachel and Eliza.

"Eliza," he said. "Did you say your name was Harris?"

Quakers, a Christian group that believes in a simple life and is against violence and war
sew, to make or repair clothes with needle and thread

"That's right," she answered nervously. She was afraid that there was bad news.

"Can I talk to you a moment, Ruth?" Simeon asked his wife.

Ruth and Simeon left the house and tears came to Eliza's eyes. Was there no peace in the world? Why couldn't those people leave Harry and her alone? Outside, Ruth and Simeon seemed to be having a serious talk.

"What is it, Simeon, bad news?" asked the wife.

"Not all bad," he answered. "There was a young man in town this morning with two women. He said his name was George Harris. He was an intelligent man, too, and sounded like the man Eliza described as her husband."

"Oh that's wonderful! She'll be so happy. I'll tell her now. What wonderful, wonderful news!"

Ruth told some of the other women the good news and walked into the room where Eliza sat with her son. When Eliza heard that George was arriving that evening she had to sit down in an armchair as she could hardly stand.

"Tonight!" she said with her eyes wide open and smiling nervously.

Moments later her eyes closed and she found herself in another world. She was asleep and in her long, peaceful sleep she dreamt of another world, full of green grass and smiling children playing in the warm sunshine. There she saw Harry and her husband walking towards her. He put his arms around her and she felt his tears falling on her neck. And then she was awake. Next to her on one side of the bed little Harry was sleeping quietly and on the other was her husband George, crying softly and watching her with a smile full of love. It was dark and a small candle was burning on the table next to the bed.

Evangeline

The Mississippi River is like no other in the world. It starts in the cold and snowy north and hurries along, carrying business up and down its length, before ending

FREE STATE
ILLINOIS
FREE STATE
INDIANA
OHIO
FREE
CINCINNATI
LOUISVILLE
MISSOURI
SLAVE
KENTUCKY
SLAVE
ARKANSAS
TENNESSEE
SLAVE
MISSISSIPPI
CLEVELAND
U S A
SLAVE
SLAVE
LOUISIANA
MISSISSIPPI
ALABAMA
RIVER
SLAVE
SLAVE
FLORIDA
ORLEANS

in the sub-tropical south, almost 3,000 miles later. But in those days the river also bore with it the tears and prayers of those whose freedom had been taken from them.

The steamboat moved slowly along the river as the evening sun reflected on the big river, carrying *cotton-bales* from the many plantations that sent the cotton down river to the markets. It is here that we find Tom, sitting behind one of these bales. Haley saw that Tom never complained and was always ready to help to load and unload the boat when it stopped at some town on the way. After a few days Haley took Tom's chains off and let him walk around wherever he wanted. When there was nothing more to do, he climbed up onto the bales and began studying his Bible.

From the boat, Tom looked out at the country around and saw the large houses of the masters. Nearby were the tiny cabins where the slaves lay down to sleep after working all day in the fields under the burning sun. Tom thought about his life in Kentucky and about his own cabin under the tall trees, surrounded by flowers. In Kentucky he saw smiling faces and heard the kind words of friends. When he looked out into the plantations he knew that Kentucky and his life there were a long way away.

Tom read very slowly, one word at a time. He didn't know how to write and the idea of sending a letter to Chloe never entered his head. Tom had his own way of finding the parts of the Bible that he enjoyed most. The marks he made in it reminded him of the good

cotton-bales, large balls of cotton

times of the past and gave him hope for the future ahead.

One of the many passengers on the boat was a young man from the wealthy St. Clare family of New Orleans. He had his five-year-old daughter with him and another woman who didn't look like his wife but seemed to know them both very well. Tom watched the little girl and thought how pretty she was. But it was not an innocent, childish prettiness. She had intelligent eyes and often had a serious look on her face as she listened to the conversations of the older people on the boat. Her face was full of life and there was nearly always a half-smile on her rosy mouth. She sang to herself as she moved around the boat and Tom thought she looked like the angels in his Bible with her gentle movements and her long white dress. Everybody on the boat had time to smile at her as she moved past them or watched them as they worked. She often sat with the slaves and then her smile would turn to sorrow as she held their chains in her little hands and saw the sadness in their eyes.

Tom, of course, had children too, and was expert at making little toys from pieces of wood or things he found. She would sit in silence watching Tom as he made her a whistle or a wooden doll.

"What's little missy's name?" he asked her after some time.

"Evangeline St. Clare," she told him, "but everybody calls me Eva. What's your name?"

"Tom, but children used to call me Uncle Tom, back in Kentucky."

"I'll call you Uncle Tom, too, because I like you," she said, smiling. "Where are you going, Uncle Tom?"

"I don't know, Miss Eva."

"Don't know?"

"No. They are going to sell me to somebody. But I don't know who."

"My Papa can buy you," she said, standing up. "I'm going to tell him."

Tom watched her running over to her father who was standing by the side of the boat as it left the landing-place. Just as she got there, she slipped and fell over the side of the boat. Her father was about to jump after her, but before he could do so a big, strong black slave had jumped in and was pulling her to the side of the boat. A hundred hands helped her back *aboard* as Tom held her up. Her father carried her to the ladies' cabin, where women ran around her, making as much fuss as possible.

The next day Tom watched Eva with her young father talking to Haley, sitting with a little notebook in front of him. It was clear that Haley was selling something. Tom could see that the young man was Eva's father. They had the same nose and mouth, only their eyes were different. Although clear and blue, Eva's eyes were a little dreamy, whereas her father's were bright and lively. He looked as if he was finding it difficult to take Haley seriously.

"Yes, yes, but what's your price? How much are you going to *cheat* me out of? Come on, name your price!" he said, looking both a little bored and amused at the same time.

"Thirteen hundred dollars would not be too much

aboard, on a ship or boat
cheat, to do something dishonest

for the man," said Haley. "I wouldn't make much for myself for that price."

"Oh, that's very good of you, you poor man," said St. Clare looking Haley in the eye. "I suppose you're selling him so cheaply because you like me so much."

"Well, your young daughter seems to like him. He's a big, strong fellow and his last master let him manage the farm."

"Hmm, that sounds bad," said St. Clare smiling to himself. "Slaves like that are too clever. They run away, I hear."

"Not this one. He's a good nigger. He always does what he's told. Back in Kentucky his folks called him a preacher."

"Oh that's just what we need," laughed St. Clare. "A family preacher. There's not much religion in the St. Clare house. The truth is, from what I hear from our white preachers, I don't think religion is any reason for putting a higher price on a man. Where I come from, church-goers are the most dishonest people you could hope to meet."

However, after some minutes Haley signed a bill of sale and was soon counting a roll of dollars. St. Clare took Eva's hand and walked over to Tom.

"Look up, Tom," he said, "and see how you like your new master."

"Thank you, Mas'r!" said Tom with tears in his eyes. "May God thank you."

"Yes, I hope he will," said St. Clare. "Now Tom, are you good with horses?"

"I've worked with horses all my life," replied Tom.

"Good. Well, you can be my driver if you promise you won't get drunk more than once a week, Tom."

"I never drink," said Tom with a serious face,

"Yes, that's what they all say," said St. Clare smiling. "You'll be the first one if it's true."

"You'll be very happy," said Eva to Tom. "Papa's always kind to everybody, only he always laughs at them."

"Thank you very much," said St. Clare walking away. "Papa's glad you think so."

Tom's New Master

Augustine St. Clare's father's family came from Canada. His mother's family were French. Both his parents came from rich families who had *emigrated* to Louisiana. Augustine was an artistic child with a sensitive character. After attending university he fell in love with a very beautiful woman from the northern states. While he was making arrangements for the wedding, he got a letter from his fiancée's *guardian*, saying that she had married another man. After some time Augustine married another woman. Everyone thought they were a perfect couple but Augustine continued to love the girl he had met at university. There was no romance in Augustine's marriage. There was always an emptiness in his heart as if a part of him had died. Marie, his wife, was too interested in herself to see this.

emigrate, to move to another country
guardian, a person who has the legal right and responsibility of taking care of someone who cannot take care of themselves

When their only child was born, instead of enjoying the happiness of motherhood, Marie became jealous of the interest that Augustine showed in their daughter.

Marie began to *complain* of headaches and spent much of the day in bed or lying on the couch. Her husband was left to supervise the house and the servants and to look after their daughter. St. Clare found all these practical problems too difficult and decided to take his daughter on a trip to Vermont in the north, and had persuaded his older cousin, Ophelia, to go back with them and help with the family.

New Orleans and New England were like two different worlds. New Orleans was hot and dusty, with big cotton plantations where rich slave-owners kept poor black slaves. There were big *colonial-style* houses and small wooden cabins without windows for the poor. New England had clean, fresh air. Its landowners were orderly and its gardens were *neat* and green. The gates and fences were always painted and everything ran *smoothly*. People worked hard and did not keep slaves. They went to church every Sunday and were careful with their money. It was peaceful and quiet. Everywhere you looked there were people working - the men in the fields, the women sewing, cooking or cleaning. In the north people spent a large part of the day keeping things clean and in order.

It was in this world that Augustine St. Clare's cou-

complain, to say that something is wrong
colonial-style, houses built in the style of the period when America was a colony. See picture, page 55.
neat, organized, not dirty
smooth, not rough; here: easy

A colonial-style house

sin, Ophelia, lived. She was forty-five years old and had never married. Her parents still treated her like a little girl. When she told them that her cousin Augustine had invited her down to New Orleans, they were very worried. The only thing they knew about the south was that it was a bad place. People were dirty, lazy and ignorant, and had very different ideas of Christianity from people in the north.

Ophelia was a tall, slim woman, neat and tidy and always dressed in plain practical clothes. If there was one thing in the world she hated, it was laziness, wasting time, and people who did things for no special reason or without an aim. Her ideas were also very simple and plain. She had a clear sense of right and wrong and did not make her life more difficult by studying more deeply than she thought was necessary. She saw the world simply, as either black or white and her serious and direct manner gave her the appearance of being very severe, not at all like her bright and romantic cousin, Augustine.

She was older than he was and was more like an aunt to him than a cousin. She loved him very much like an older sister loves a younger brother and her heart became softer when she looked at him. This was why she had decided to take the big step of going south to help her cousin take care of his house and family.

Even on the boat, where there was never much to do, Ophelia kept herself busy, organizing things and keeping everything tidy, including Eva. Half an hour before the boat arrived in New Orleans she was sitting on top of all their luggage making sure that it was ready to be taken off the boat. When the boat finally stopped, she refused to let other people help with the bags and waited instead for Augustine to finish a long conversation with another passenger. In the end they were the last ones to get off the boat.

"That's better," said St. Clare. "I hate being pushed along by all those people hurrying to get off."

When they reached the St. Clare house, Tom found it difficult to believe what he was seeing. They went in through a gate and came to a large square *courtyard*. In the middle there was a big fountain surrounded by

courtyard, a large open area on the inside of a castle or a large house

grass, flowering plants and orange trees. The house itself was a mixture of French and Spanish styles with white walls and arched galleries that ran all around the courtyard. It was the most beautiful and romantic house Tom had ever seen. Eva was happy to be home again.

"Isn't it a lovely house, Aunt Ophelia?" she said. "I think it's beautiful."

"Yes, it's pretty," said her aunt, almost smiling. "But it looks very old and *heathenish* to me."

As they got closer to the door a crowd of servants - men, women and children - came running out of the front door towards them. A young and very fashionably dressed mulatto man sent them all back into the house and made a *speech* of welcome.

"Yes, yes, thank you, Adolphe," said St. Clare. "Now ask somebody to take our bags in, will you?"

Eva was already inside kissing and embracing her mother who was lying on a couch.

"That'll do. Take care, child! Stop it! You make my head ache," said the mother, kissing her coldly.

As St. Clare came in through the door, her eyes moved from him to Ophelia, who followed. Marie received her with cold politeness. Eva now ran over to a very large black woman standing in the door.

"*Mammy*!" she cried, kissing her again and again. The black woman smiled, picked her up and hugged her more like a mother than a servant. Then Eva jumped down and kissed all the other servants one after

heathenish, uncivilized, having no religion
speech, a formal and usually prepared talk given by one person to others
Mammy, a name used when talking to older black women servants

another. Ophelia watched all this in *disgust.* Kissing them was more than she cared for.

St. Clare took Tom by the arm and walked him over to where his wife sat on her couch. Tom was still amazed by the beauty of the house with all its expensive furniture and ornaments. He was almost afraid to put his feet on the floor.

"Darling, look what I've brought you," he told his wife. "This is Tom, our new driver."

"Hmm," she said, not looking too pleased at what she saw. "I hope he doesn't drink as much as the last one."

The well-dressed Adolphe then took Tom to the room that was to be his bedroom.

"Where have you been? You said you were coming two weeks ago," the young wife complained. "How could you leave me here on my own when I feel so ill? I could have died here but you don't care. You never think of my feelings."

"I wrote you that I couldn't come until today. You know why," said St. Clare.

"I've had my headaches ever since you left," continued the wife.

"*Juniper* tea is very good for headaches," said Ophelia. "Back up north we always drink juniper tea when we have headaches."

"You must be tired yourself," said St. Clare to Ophelia. "Mammy! Take this lady and show her to her room. She is tired and needs a rest."

disgust, strong dislike
juniper, a kind of fruit

The Opinions of a Southern *Mistress*

The morning after St. Clare's return, the family sat down to Sunday breakfast.

"Well, Marie," said St. Clare. "Here is our practical cousin Ophelia who will take care of the house for you."

"I'm sure she's welcome. The first thing she needs to know is that we mistresses are the slaves down here."

"Why do we keep slaves, Mama?" asked Evangeline, with large, serious eyes.

"I don't know I'm sure. If you ask me, we could let them all go today. I believe it's worrying about them that makes me feel so ill," said her mother, putting her hand to her head.

"Oh, you know that's not true, dear," St. Clare said. "How can you say that? Where would we be without Mammy?"

"Mammy! She only thinks of herself, just like all the other black women."

"Yes, *selfishness* is a dreadful fault," said St. Clare seriously. "But I wouldn't say she was selfish. After all, she wakes up in the middle of the night to look after you when you have your headaches. Why don't you let one of the other girls take her place?"

"You know how I dislike having strange hands touching me. Anyway, if Mammy really cared about me, she'd wake up more quickly."

Ophelia just sat straight in her chair during this conversation, being sure not to say anything. Marie con-

mistress, here, the wife of the master
selfishness, thinking only of yourself, not of others

tinued to complain about her servant.

"And she is selfish. When I got married and came here, Mammy wanted to stay back on my father's farm with that husband of hers. I told her to find another man but she wouldn't. I wish now that I'd insisted on it. She's always worrying about that man."

"Does she have any children?" Ophelia asked.

"Yes, two, I think," Marie went on. "But we didn't need children down here. They had to stay on my father's farm. She must have known she'd never see them again. They were such dirty little things as well. She'd go back there tomorrow if she could. Never mind about me. She never thinks of anyone but herself."

Ophelia looked over to where St. Clare sat in silence. She saw how angry and uncomfortable he looked.

"I wish some of your northern servants could see what a good life they have. They get tea and coffee every day. I give Mammy my old dresses and she was never whipped more than once or twice. St. Clare lets them live almost as they please. I'm tired of talking to him about it."

"And I'm tired of hearing about it," said her husband and began to read his newspaper.

"Couldn't I take care of you one night, Mama?" asked Eva, putting her head on her mother's arm.

"No, child, what nonsense!" said her mother. "What a strange girl you are."

"But I don't think Mammy's very well. She always says she's got a headache."

"Oh, you know her, always complaining, just like the rest of them," said Marie and looked over at Ophelia. "You watch them. If you give them too much freedom, the first thing they do is complain. Make them work harder, that's what I say. Nobody knows what I have to put up with."

St. Clare had had enough. He folded his paper and walked out of the door.

"That's just like him," said his wife after he had left. "Every time I talk about my health he walks away. He should be happy. I'm not the kind of wife who spends all her days complaining. He doesn't know how lucky he is."

After a while, Marie began to tell Ophelia how she managed the house, which Ophelia found a little difficult to follow.

"And that's that. I'm sure you'll be able to manage next time I have one of my headaches. And *keep an eye on* Eva. She's a strange child. Not like me at all," said her mother. Ophelia silently hoped not. "To be honest, I don't understand why her father lets her play with those little Negro children. He seems to think more of them than he does of me. Let me tell you something. When we married, I brought all my servants with me. I let St. Clare manage them but they are mine, not his. He refuses to *punish* them and you see what happens. They need more control. They are just like grown-up children."

"I don't know anything about it, thank the Lord!" said Ophelia, who did not want to take sides in a family argument. "But we are all God's creatures and are all equal, don't you think?"

"Not at all!" said Marie angrily. "They are not like

keep an eye on, to watch closely
punish, to make people suffer or hurt them, because they have done something wrong

us at all. They have different feelings from us. St. Clare tried to tell me that Mammy loved her chidren as much as I love Eva. How stupid! How could it be the same for Mammy as for me? They are not the same as us. How could they love those dirty little black babies? I tell you, if I had control, I'd let them know who was in charge."

Fighting for Freedom

The next day was a busy one at the Quaker house. George, Eliza and little Harry were to begin their dangerous journey to Canada that night. George and Eliza were sitting in their little room, talking.

"When we get to Canada," said Eliza, "I'll make dresses and find work washing or cooking. Together we'll be all right."

"Yes, Eliza, the important thing is that we have each other and our son. You know, this is the first time I have ever been able to feel that this family is **mine**. And that's the best thing a man can have. People sometimes forget what a blessing it is. I feel as rich as a man can be."

"Yes, my love, but we are not out of danger yet. We are not yet in Canada," said Eliza.

"I know," said her husband, "but I can almost smell the air of freedom and it makes me strong."

Outside, the Quakers were standing around a Quaker brother who had just arrived. Phineas Fletcher was not like the other men in the community. He was *alert*

alert, keen, lively

and sharp-eyed. He didn't have the peaceful and unworldly manner of the others. He had not been born a Quaker but had married into the community after falling in love with one of the women there. He had given up his life as a hunter and moved into the village with his wife. He found it difficult to change his lifestyle, though, and still had the hardness and sharp eyes of his earlier days.

Eliza opened the door and George could see there was bad news.

"Our friend Phineas brings important news," said Simeon.

"I was in the tavern on the old road last night," Phineas told George, "when a group of seven or eight strangers at the next table started talking about Quakers. I listened and heard them say they were going to the Quaker community where there were some runaway slaves, one of whom they were going to take back to his master in Kentucky. They were going to take his wife down to Orleans and sell her. The boy was to be given back to the trader who'd bought him."

Phineas looked around at the other Quakers. "So what are we going to do, then?"

"I know what I'm going to do," said George and took two pistols from his bag.

Phineas looked at the shocked faces of the peace-loving Quakers. "Do you see what's going to happen, Simeon?" he asked.

"I pray it won't come to that."

"I don't want to involve any of you in this," said George. "It's my fight, not yours. If you'll lend me your carriage, that will be enough."

"I think I can help you drive the carriage," said

Phineas. "You can fight if you want but I know the road better than you do."

"I'll only use these guns to protect myself if we are attacked. The only thing I ask in this country is to be let alone, and I'll leave peacefully. But my sister was sold in that market down in Orleans and I know what they are sold as. Am I to stand by and see them take my wife and sell her when God has given me a pair of strong arms to defend her? I'll fight to the last breath before I let them take my wife and son!"

Everybody in the community helped to prepare them for the journey. In two hours George, Eliza and Harry were ready. By the evening, they had all eaten well and were ready to leave. Before they left, Simeon spoke to them all.

"Remember this," he said. "Sometimes you might ask yourself where God is when you see so much evil. But it is often those who have least that God chooses for his Kingdom. Put your trust in him and he will make everything right."

The night was clear and full of stars when they left. Phineas sat with George and drove the horses on along the dusty road, up and down hills and between the rocks. At the back of the carriage, the others sat in fear and silence. It was early in the morning when George heard the sound of a horse coming. Phineas pulled up.

"That sounds like Michael's horse," said Phineas. The Quakers had sent their best rider as a messenger. After a few minutes the horse came up to the carriage.

"What's the news, Michael?" asked Phineas.

"There are eight men coming just behind me and they've all been drinking. Listen!"

They stood in silence, listening. After a few seconds

the wind carried the sound of galloping horses towards them. Phineas jumped back into his seat and *lashed* the horses to a gallop towards some high rocks. Behind them the sound of horses and men's voices grew louder. Eliza prayed and held Harry close to her. George took his pistol in desperation. Phineas knew where he was heading for. He quickly got the carriage up to the big rocks. When he got there, he got the others out and ran with them up to the top of the rocks. There was only one way to the top along a narrow old hunters' path which Phineas remembered from his younger days. When they got to the top, the horsemen were already stopping their horses and deciding what to do next.

"It looks like the niggers are hiding up in the rocks," said one of them to Tom Loker.

"Yeah. So let's go and get them down. Follow me, boys, there's a path over there."

"Be careful, Tom," said his friend, Marks. "They might shoot from behind the rocks."

"That's typical of you, Marks. Always saving your own skin. Don't worry - them niggers won't shoot at no-one. They're too scared."

At this point George stood on top of one of the rocks and shouted down to Tom Loker and his men.

"Who are you and what do you want?" he asked.

"We want some runaway niggers," said Loker. Aren't you George Harris, that belongs to Mr Harris of Kentucky?"

"Yes, I'm George Harris but I'm nobody's slave. I'm a free man standing on free ground and my wife and

lash, to hit with a whip

child are mine, and as free as I am. If any of you doesn't agree, you can come up here. But the first one who *comes within range* is a dead man."

The other men stood and listened but Marks took out his gun and pointed it up the rock at George. When he fired, the bullet flew just past George's ear and into a tree behind him.

"You get just as much money for him dead as alive in Kentucky," he said coolly, wiping his pistol on his sleeve.

George jumped back behind the rock. He saw Tom Loker leading the others along the narrow path. George pointed one of his pistols at Tom and fired a bullet into the big man's side. But that only stopped him for a second or two. Holding his side he jumped up over the rocks and almost into the group when the strong arms of Phineas pushed Loker over a rock. The big man fell down over the rocks and stones until he lay groaning thirty feet below. The others ran to help him up and tried to carry him to his horse. Marks, though, was already gone for help, as he said. But Loker knew differently.

"Oh, I hope he's not dead," said Eliza, who had stood watching.

"Why?" said Phineas. "He got what he asked for. Look, they're leaving him there."

It was true. The men tried to get Loker onto the horse but he was too heavy for them. Instead they got onto their horses and rode away.

"Oh, the poor man! We must go and help him," said Eliza.

come within range, to be at shooting distance

The group came down from the rocks and walked over to where Tom Loker lay on the ground. After being treated by Phineas, he was lifted into the carriage. "He'll be all right," said Phineas.

"I hope so," said George. "I never wanted to kill a man."

"We'll take him up to a farm along the road where he'll be looked after."

So the group continued their journey and left the injured man in the care of good people, in a bed that was cleaner than any he had ever slept in. There he was looked after until he was well enough to leave.

Life in the St. Clare House

As the weeks and months went by, Tom and Ophelia, each in their different ways, began to take control of life in the St. Clare household in New Orleans. Tom began to take over some of Adolphe's work. Adolphe, like his master, never worried much about money and Tom was shocked to see how much waste there was everywhere. Little by little Tom began to get things in order, just as he had done when he lived in Kentucky. St. Clare trusted him and let him take charge of all the marketing and household expenses.

Tom thought that his new master was a sad person who ought to take more care of himself. After a night out drinking with his friends, St. Clare had to be helped home. Tom decided to speak.

"Mas'r," he said, holding his hat in his hands. "I feel very bad today."

"Why's that, Tom? What's the problem?" said St.

Clare putting down his coffee cup.

"I always thought you would be good to everybody."

"Well, am I not?" asked St. Clare.

"Yes, but why are you not good to yourself, Mas'r?" Tom fell on his knees and St. Clare saw the big man was crying.

"Poor fool. Get up, Tom. I'm not worth crying for. I don't know why I go to those parties. I've always hated myself for going. But I promise you, you'll never again see me like that. I promise you."

Ophelia was just as determined as Tom to bring order into the family. It was clear that St. Clare's wife Marie was not a good housewife. She took no interest in the daily running of the house or in the training of her servants. Ophelia found complete chaos in the kitchen. Dinah, the cook, didn't know where to find anything and a lot of time was wasted opening cupboards and pulling out kitchen drawers to find a fish knife or a cake tray. For a woman like Ophelia this was the worst kitchen she had ever seen. When she told St. Clare about the confusion in the kitchen, he answered calmly, he did not seem to be very worried.

"Yes, I know, but Dinah always finds things and the work gets done in the end. Dinah and the other servants are quite happy about the way things are run."

This was true. Dinah was very *put out* when Ophelia began to clear up. It was also a shock for the servants. They had never seen white ladies doing that kind of work. They tried to stop her when she started to take old vegetables out of cupboards and wash dirty pans and plates. After a few days, though, the kitchen was a

put out, annoyed, angry

different place and Ophelia felt a lot happier with it. But the servants liked the old ways. They gave her no help at all.

Tom, to be honest, did not have a very hard life at the St. Clare house and had time to spend with little Eva, who became his closest friend there. The difference in their ages did not seem to affect their friendship. Tom was a simple man with a big heart. He found it hard to understand why there was such a big difference between rich and poor, and why some people wanted to live so differently from the people in the Bible. It was this book, the only book he had, that made life worth living.

He *admired* his young friend. Tom thought she looked like one of the angels in his Bible. It always surprised him to see such a young person take an interest in other people and their problems. But sometimes her interest made her very unhappy. She often told her father that she had a heavy heart. Then both St. Clare and Tom would worry about her and do their best to take her mind off the world's problems.

Some months after Tom came to New Orleans, he missed his home so much that he tried to write a letter to Chloe in Kentucky. He sat in his little room and with great difficulty tried to form words from the few letters he had learned. Eva came in and looked over his shoulder.

"What are you drawing, Uncle Tom?" she asked.

"I'm trying to write a letter to my wife, Miss Eva, and my children," he said, "but I'm not sure I can."

"I wish I could help you, Uncle Tom," Eva said. "Last

admire, to think highly of someone

year I knew all the letters but I'm afraid I've forgotten them now."

So they sat together and slowly filled a page with writing. It looked very much like a letter when it was finished.

"Oh, Uncle Tom, it looks beautiful," Eva said at last. "How pleased your wife and children will be! I'm going to ask Papa to let you go back, some time."

"They said they'd send down money to buy me back," said Tom, taking a coin out from under his shirt. "Young Mas'r George gave me this silver dollar and promised me he'd come for me one day."

At this point St. Clare walked in looking for his daughter.

"What's that you're doing there?" he asked.

"Uncle Tom's writing a letter and I'm helping him," said Eva. "His mistress is going to send money down to buy him back."

"I think it would be better if I helped you, Tom. I'll do it when I come home. But now I want you to get the horses ready."

St. Clare had heard before about kind owners making such promises to their servants, so they wouldn't be so frightened at being sold. He knew, too, that this never happened and that slaves never returned to their families and friends once they were sold. He kept his promise, though. He wrote Tom's letter for him and made sure it was sent.

When the letter arrived in Kentucky it caused a lot of *excitement*, especially for Aunt Chloe. She began to

excitement, a strong feeling. Here, of happiness

make plans to earn enough money to buy her husband back.

"I was *wondering*, Missis," she said nervously the next day, "if it was possible..."

"If what's possible, Chloe?" Mrs Shelby asked.

"Well, Sally's a good cook now - almost as good as me with most things, and I was thinking maybe we should let her take charge of the kitchen now."

"We couldn't do that, Chloe. We love your cooking. What would you do anyway, if Sally was doing all the cooking?"

"I was thinking," said Chloe nervously, "that maybe you could *hire* me out to somebody. I heard they were looking for somebody at the cake-shop in Louisville. Maybe I could save some of the money to go and buy Tom back."

"Well, Chloe, I'll be sorry to see you go, but I think it's a fine idea. And I'll save every cent of your wages for your husband's return."

"Oh thank you Missis. You're so good! That cake-shop pays four dollars a week. How many weeks are there in a year, Missis?"

"Fifty-two, Chloe," said Mrs Shelby.

"So how long would it take me to work it off?" asked Chloe, holding her hands together and smiling widely. A cloud passed over Mrs Shelby's heart on hearing this question. "Well, four or five years, Chloe. But I'll add something to it."

That same day, Chloe packed the few things she was going to need in the big town and made arrangements

wonder, to think to yourself
hire, to take money for letting somebody use something

for the other servants to look after her children while she was gone. When everything was ready, she asked Mrs Shelby's son George to write a letter to Tom, telling him of her plan.

The Flower *Fades*

It was two years since Tom had left Kentucky and in that time his friendship with Eva had grown stronger and stronger. As she grew older, her reading got better and she began to take a great interest in reading the Bible to Tom. At first she read just to please Tom, but as time went by, she began to see the stories in a more personal way and read them with feeling and imagination. Tom was often lost in the pictures that her storytelling made him see. Eva sometimes lost herself in the stories too, often stopping to look out of the window or up in the sky.

"Uncle Tom, I'm going there," she said one day.

"Where, Miss Eva?"

"Up there," she said, standing up and pointing her finger to the sky. "To the spirits. I'm going there soon, Uncle Tom."

Tom saw how the sunlight shone on her soft, golden hair. Tom felt a heavy sadness in his heart. How thin her hands were now and how pale her skin. Tom had already noticed the feverish cheek and the eyes that burned too brightly. He had heard Eva coughing and seen how none of Ophelia's medicines seemed to help, but this was the first time the idea entered his head that Eva, his beloved Eva, was dying.

fade, to lose colour

Ophelia had been the first to notice but St. Clare did not want to believe her. He would not even talk about it.

"Don't be silly, cousin," he said, picking up his paper. "She's only growing. Children always get tired when they grow quickly. You'll see. She'll get better and be healthier and stronger than the rest of us."

But then he began to see that Ophelia was right. He grew fonder than ever of his only child. As time went by her mind seemed to grow faster than her body. St.

Clare was often surprised at how deeply his daughter thought about the world around her. He watched as she sat with the servants' children. Although she laughed as much as before, she no longer took part in their games. She was becoming a young woman, and her father saw a new seriousness in her eyes.

"Mama," she once said. "Why don't we teach our servants to read?"

"What a question, child! People never do."

"Why not?"

"Because it's no use to them. They don't work any better, and they're not made for anything else."

"But they should read the Bible, Mama, don't you think?"

"Other people can read the Bible to them when they want to hear it," said her mother impatiently.

"But I think people should read the Bible when they want to, in their free time. Mammy would love to read the Bible, she always tells me."

"Listen, child, when you're a little older you won't have time to worry about servants," said her mother and opened a little box on her bedroom table. She pulled a diamond necklace from it and showed it to Eva. "This is the necklace I wore when I first went to a dance and I'm going to give it to you when you go to your first *ball*."

"It must have cost a lot of money," said Eva thoughtfully. "If I had it I'd sell it and buy a house in the free states and take all our people there. I'd hire teachers and teach them to read and write."

At this point Eva was stopped by her mother's laugh-

ball, a very formal party where people dance

ing. "Start a school! Now don't be so silly, Eva, you're only a child. You don't know anything about these things, so be quiet now. Your talking makes my head ache."

Marie always had a headache when the conversation did not please her. But Eva quietly walked away to see Mammy, who was about to get the first reading lesson of her life.

As the months passed, Eva's health got worse and worse. Her father decided at last to call the doctor. Marie did not believe that Eva was ill. What was worse, she was angry with her husband for being more interested in Eva's health than in her's. Ophelia also tried to make Marie aware of her daughter's illness but she only managed to make her more interested in her own headaches and continued sickness. When it finally became clear that Eva was extremely ill, Marie St. Clare could only think and talk about how unfortunate she was.

"I always knew this was going to happen," she told her husband. "I knew I was going to be an unhappy mother and now my only child is going to be taken from me. How unlucky I am."

"You shouldn't talk like that." said St. Clare angrily. "You ought not to give up hope at once."

"Oh, you don't feel what a mother feels. After all I have been through. It's too much for me."

Marie now took Eva's illness more seriously, and spent so much time showing everybody around her how sad she was that Eva cried in pity for her mother's *distress*. Eva herself was cheerful. The stories she read

distress, great unhappiness or fear

with Tom seemed to give her hope and she believed that, after her death, she would go to heaven. But she was sad for the loved ones she was leaving behind. And she felt she needed to do something good for the poor and hungry of the world and help those whose only 'wrong' was to be born with black and not white skin.

"I know I'm going to die soon," she told her father one afternoon as she sat on his knee.

"Now, now, child, you mustn't talk like that," he answered, holding back the tears in his eyes.

"You know it's true, Daddy," she said, "I am going soon. I'm not afraid or low-spirited. If it were not for the people I leave behind, I should be perfectly happy. But I wish all our people were free, Papa."

"Don't you think they are content, Eva?"

"They are now, but what would become of them if anything happened to you? Mama wouldn't look after them like you do and Ophelia doesn't know what to do with them. People do horrible things to their slaves. I remember those poor slaves on the boat we took down the Mississippi when we bought Tom. I remember their sad faces and the stories of their families that they'd never see again. Isn't there any way, Papa, to make all slaves free?"

"You know, my child, that I hate slavery with all my heart. So do many other people. But I don't know what is to be done about it."

"But you are good at talking, Papa, and you are a kind man. I'm sure you could change things after I'm dead," she said.

"Dead! Oh please don't talk like that, Eva. You are all I have in this world."

"But think of Tom and his family and Mammy who

hasn't seen her family for many years. They have nobody in the world, either. Promise me one thing, Daddy."

"Yes, my child, of course, but don't talk of death, please."

"Let Tom have his freedom as soon as .... when I am gone," she said, turning her face towards her father's.

"Yes, dear, of course, whatever you want."

St. Clare held his weak daughter closer to him and soon felt her fall asleep. For hours he sat there holding his dying child's body close to his heart. As he sat there, St. Clare saw his whole life, as in a dream. He carried his child to her bedroom and sang her to sleep.

Death

Eva very rarely left the bedroom now. She was sometimes able to step onto the verandah, but as she grew weaker, she spent more and more time lying on a couch by the open window, surrounded by the flowers that her family and the servants took her every day. She was never alone. Her father and Ophelia spent most of the day with her. Her mother was often there, too, but seemed unable to stop herself from crying every time she came into the room. The servants came to visit as often as their work around the house would let them, and Tom filled two vases with flowers every morning.

There was also a little servant girl, Topsy, that Eva had become good friends with. Topsy was not very well liked by the other servants because she was always stealing things from them. St. Clare had bought her from her last owner as a present for Ophelia. He thought it would be amusing to see how his cousin from the north would educate this little slave-girl who had no mother or father and a history of stealing. In fact, Ophelia found it impossible. The little girl's last owner had hit her every time she did something wrong, and told her so many times that she was bad, that she now was sure of it, and seemed quite happy not to be loved by anyone. Ophelia tried as hard as she could to give the child *discipline* and respect but without result. But all that changed one day when Eva told Topsy that she loved her. This was the first time anybody had ever told Topsy they loved her. All her life she had been beaten and punished and locked up without food, but not once had anybody told her they liked her. From that day on, Topsy was a different child, and Eva's very good friend.

One day Topsy walked into the bedroom with some flowers for Eva.

"Now where did you steal those from, you bad litle nigger?" said Marie, slapping the child.

"Why, Missis, they're for Eva, I picked them," said the little girl and began to walk out.

"Oh, come back, Topsy," said Eva. "They're beautiful. Let me keep them, Mama. Topsy picked them for me."

"You have enough flowers already. Your room is full of them."

"Topsy, bring them here. They're beautiful!" said Eva.

"Well, if that's what you want," said her mother angrily. "Topsy, do what your mistress tells you!"

Topsy came back and put the flowers on the table

discipline, training which gives self-control

next to Eva's bed. A tear rolled down her cheek.

"Don't you think that Topsy's a good girl now, Mama?" Eva asked when Topsy left the room.

"She'll have to try much harder before **she** gets to be good," said her mother.

"But poor Topsy," said Eva seriously. "Everything has always been against her. It must be a difficult life. She doesn't have the good life that I've had."

"Oh, dear, how hot it is," said her mother, *yawning*.

"Do you think Topsy will go to heaven one day, Mama?" Eva asked.

"Topsy? What a foolish idea. But I suppose she could."

"But God is her father, too, isn't he, Mama?"

"Well, possibly," said Marie, putting her hand to her head. "You should be glad that God has given us our advantages. I'm certainly glad for them."

"But I'd like God to come down and save them all so that they can be free, like I am," said Eva.

"I want some of my hair cut off, it makes my head hot and it's too long," Eva said after a while. "I can give some to my friends while I am still able to give it away myself."

So that afternoon Eva had her golden-brown curls cut off by her aunt Ophelia while St. Clare sat and watched her sadly. When her hair was short and all of her long curls lay on the bed in front of her, she asked her father to tell the servants to come in. One by one they came into the bedroon and stood silently watching the young girl separating the pieces of hair. They

yawn, to open the mouth wide and deeply breathe in and out, usually when tired or bored

saw better than before how weak she was, how red her *cheeks* were from the illness and how slowly her eyes moved from one to the other. But Eva was not sad. She smiled weakly at them and finally broke the silence.

"I've cut my hair so that you can all have a *lock* of it. I want you all to remember when you look at my hair that I have gone to heaven and that one day you'll be there, too. I want you to remember that I love you and that I'll be waiting for you."

Every servant in the house walked up to the dying girl and took a lock of her hair, crying as they did so. Some of them kissed her on the head, others said short prayers. Ophelia signalled for them all to leave. Tom and Mammy stayed a little longer. When they had gone, Ophelia saw that Topsy was still there.

"Come on you, out you go!" Ophelia said pushing the girl through the door.

"Oh, Miss Eva, please." she said, stopping in the door. "I know I'm a bad girl but won't you give me one, too?"

"Yes, Topsy, this is for you. There. Every time you look at it, remember that I love you and want you to be good."

"I **am** trying, Miss Eva," she said, crying. "But it's difficult."

"Jesus knows it's hard for you, Topsy. He'll help you."

In the days that followed Eva grew weaker and weaker. St. Clare had less and less time for his wife and they hardly spoke to each other. Tom sometimes carried the

cheek, the side of the face
lock, some pieces of hair

girl out to sit on the verandah and began to sleep outside her bedroom door at night. Ophelia, too, stayed up all night and gave the girl medicine when she needed it. It was in the middle of the night when Ophelia woke Tom and told him to run for the doctor. She woke St. Clare and told him to come at once. A few minutes later the doctor arrived and took one look at Eva. Everybody could see from the look he gave St. Clare that these were the last moments of her life. St. Clare held his daughter's cold hands and spoke in her ear, "Eva, darling. Do you know me?"

Eva's eyes opened and she smiled and put her arms around her father's neck, "Dear Papa," she said and her eyes slowly closed again. Her arms dropped from his neck and her face filled with pain. St. Clare took Tom's hand as he watched the pain in his daughter's face. "Oh, Tom, Tom, this is killing me," he cried. Tom looked up to the night sky and then back at Eva's face.

"Look Mas'r. It's over now."

St. Clare looked again at Eva and saw a peaceful smile appear. "Eva, what do you see?"

"Love ... Peace!" she said slowly and then, with a sigh was gone forever.

The Death of Hope

Eva's death affected the people in the house in different ways. St. Clare himself was perhaps the one who seemed to be the least affected by it. He was more serious around the house but in town people saw the same smiling, well-dressed, thinking man that they had always known. But this was all on the *surface*.

"Still waters run deep," Ophelia told Marie one day. He never cried and found it difficult to talk about Eva.

His wife was another story. Day and night the servants could hear her crying. They had very little time to think of their own sadness as she kept them awake at night with her *moaning*. She said she was dying and some of the servants believed her and sent for the doctor. St. Clare watched his wife's behaviour with very little interest. He was so lost in his own thoughts.

Tom and Ophelia could see the sadness in St. Clare's eyes, in his movements, in the way he spoke. Tom stayed close to him all day and was the only person St. Clare could talk to. He had lost his only reason for living. Tom saw the lost look in his master's eyes.

"If Mas'r could look up to the sky where Eva is, up to the Lord Jesus," Tom told him.

"I look up all the time, Tom, but I don't see anything. I wish I did. I want to believe the Bible, but I can't. No, Tom, there is nothing else. No heaven, no God, no Eva, nothing."

"You must believe, Mas'r," said Tom. "When I was sold and was taken away from my wife and children, it was the Lord that helped me. I knew he was watching me and was going to help me. If you believe in Him, I know you won't feel lonely again."

Tom began to say some of the prayers that he and Eva used to say together. He spoke them with so much feeling that his voice seemed to carry him away to another world, to a world that was closer to Eva.

surface, the top or outside part of something
moaning, the noise of someone crying

St. Clare found it difficult to fill his time now that his daughter was gone. He found no reason for doing anything. The house and land would have been hers and there was now no reason to take care of it. He began to think more about his servants and how he could improve their lives. He decided it was the right time to start taking steps to give Tom his freedom.

"Tom," he said, "I'm going to make you a free man. So pack your *trunk*, because soon you'll be back in Kentucky."

"Oh, thank you, Lord," said Tom, looking to the sky.

"Why, Tom, you surprise me. Has life been so hard for you here?"

"No Mas'r, it's not that. It's being a free man. That's what makes me so happy."

"But don't you think life was better here than if you had been a free man?"

"No, sir. There's nothing can make a man so happy as freedom. Mas'r has been good to me. But I'd rather have poor clothes, poor house, poor everything, and have them mine, and not another man's."

"Well, I suppose that's natural. In a few weeks you'll be leaving me."

"No, Mas'r. I won't leave you as long as you're in trouble."

"Trouble, Tom? When will my trouble be over?"

"When Mas'r St. Clare is a Christian," said Tom.

The others in the house were also deeply affected by Eva's death. Mammy, especially, was heart-broken. She began to forget things and was careless with her work, which only made Marie angrier with her.

trunk, suitcase

Ophelia began to lose her northern coldness and became softer, more gentle. She grew closer to little Topsy, who felt the loss of her only real friend as much as anyone. Ophelia began to see that Topsy was not only a little slave-girl. She was a young child with a natural need for love, care and education. Topsy slowly started to change for the better.

One day Ophelia told St. Clare that she wanted him to give Topsy to her, so she could take the girl back north with her where she could be free. St. Clare was amazed. But Ophelia would not do it until St. Clare signed the official papers that gave her the right to take Topsy wherever she wanted.

"There you are," he said, when he had signed. "She's yours."

"She's not mine," said Ophelia. "Only God has a right to give her to me. But I can protect her now."

Ophelia then asked St. Clare what arrangements he had made for the other servants in case of his death.

"It's not an easy matter to decide," said St. Clare. "What would become of them? Suppose that tomorrow we gave all the slaves in the southern states their freedom. What would they do with it? No one here would help them to get an education or to find work for themselves. They'd have to move up north where people are interested in work. And then what would happen? You northern people, who spend so much money sending *missionaries* to Africa, would never let the black man enter your churches. How many in the free states would give a black man a job as a mechanic, or send a black girl like Topsy to school with white children? How

missionary, a person who is sent to another country to teach religion

many families would open their doors and let a black man sleep in their house? You see, cousin, it is easy to say how bad we are in the south but is the *prejudice* of the free north any better?"

"We can only try," said Ophelia, "just as I'm going to try with Topsy. I can see the good in these people and how much they have to give us. I'm sure we can show people in the north how to do things, little by little."

St. Clare felt he needed to take a walk after this conversation. Tom saw him walk through the gate and had a strange feeling of sadness and hope. Sadness for the look on his master's face as he left the house and hope for the future. He began to plan the day when he would see his wife and family again. It was now three years since he last saw or heard from them. He sat there thinking about them in the warm southern evening and prayed to his God for the future.

He was almost asleep in the garden when he suddenly heard voices outside the gate. He ran over and opened it. A group of men came in, carrying the body of his master, covered in blood. Tom helped the men carry St. Clare into the house and lay him on a couch. St. Clare had been reading a newspaper in one of the town's bars when two drunk men started fighting. St. Clare tried to stop the fight and got a *fatal stab* in the side with a knife. The doctor was called, and he tried to stop the blood. But St. Clare was losing his strength. He opened his eyes and laid his hand on Tom, who was kneeling beside him.

prejudice, opinion not based on reason
fatal, causing death
stab, to injure with a knife

"Tom," he said, "poor Tom. I'm dying, Tom."

"Would you like a preacher, sir," the doctor asked him.

"No. Pray for me, Tom."

And Tom did pray as hard as he had ever prayed in his life. When he finished praying, St. Clare took Tom's hand. Moving closer to him, Tom heard him say, "I'm going home, Tom. Home at last." As he said his last words, his strength left him and he lay completely still, smiling like a man who had finally found peace.

The Unprotected

Augustine St. Clare's death came as such a terrible shock that for weeks everyone walked around the house as if in a nightmare. Marie broke down totally, and appeared to have lost control of herself. Ophelia or one of the servants sometimes found her lying on the floor where she had fallen. Only Ophelia was able to keep some form of self-control and saw that the young *widow's* sadness was real. She did her best to keep the house working and the servants busy.

She was helped by Tom, who was less sad than most of the others. He knew that his dead master had gone to a better place and was up there somewhere above the clouds with his daughter.

The funeral came and went, and everybody began to think "What is to happen now?" Ophelia began to think of her return to the north, especially when she saw how Marie treated the servants, now that all the authority was in her hands. Marie started to punish the servants and have them whipped. Instead of their laughter and friendly talk, there was now silence and fear. Ophelia tried as hard as she could to help and defend the poor slaves but Marie had the power and nothing would stop her from using it.

At first Tom was happy to help around the house. But soon he began to think once again about the freedom that his late master had promised him.

"Miss Ophelia," he said, "Master St. Clare promised me my freedom before he died. I was wondering if you could talk to Missis. She might feel like letting me go,

widow, the living wife of a dead man

as it was her husband's plan to do."

"Well, Tom," she said, with a heavy heart, "You know I'll do what I can. But you've seen how she punishes the others. I can't give you much hope, I'm afraid."

When Ophelia went to ask Marie about Tom's future, she received a worse answer than she had expected.

"I'm sorry, Ophelia," said Marie. "It's too late. My lawyer has already written the papers. I'm selling the house and everything in it, including Tom and all the other slaves."

"But St. Clare promised him his freedom," Ophelia insisted.

"St. Clare is not here to worry about it, is he? It's my house, Ophelia, and I'd be glad if you let me manage it as I want to. Negroes are always complaining. What they need is good, strong masters to stop them from getting lazy and drinking too much. Freedom would be no good for them at all."

The argument continued, but Marie did not change her point of view. In fact, the more they argued, the more decided she became to sell Tom and the others. The conversation ended when Marie covered her face with her handkerchief and seemed to cry. Almost immediately she shouted for one of the servants to bring the medicine she took for her headaches. Ophelia went back to her room and wrote at once to Mrs Shelby asking for her help for Tom.

The next day Tom and six other servants were taken to the slave market where they were to be sold that same day.

Sold Again

The slave market in New Orleans was open every day for trade. Hundreds of human beings were bought and sold every week. The prices the sellers got for their "property" depended on many things - age, health, strength and education, for example. Tom was not a young man any more but he was still strong and hard-working. He was sold for a good price and was put shortly after in the back of a cart with the other slaves his new master had bought at the market. The others were two young men who were bought because they could work hard and the other was a young girl of fifteen, who sat quietly crying. Tom could see by her clothes that she had worked in the house of a rich family. Her soft hands told him that she had never worked on a farm, and Tom knew the cross she wore showed that she was a Christian. At the market Tom had seen the girl being taken away from her mother. The mother had begun to pray as her daughter was taken from her, perhaps never to see her again. They sat in sad silence, wondering what kind of life was waiting for them. Their new master, Mr Simon Legree was a hard-looking man with strong shoulders, a round, *bald* head and very cruel eyes. He was the owner of a cotton plantation up the Red River and Tom and the other slaves were already preparing their minds for a life of hard work and few of the comforts Tom had enjoyed at the St. Clare house.

From the cart the slaves were taken to a wooden boat on the Red River. There they were chained

bald, with no hair

together with four other slaves Legree had bought at another market. Once the boat began to move up river, Legree walked over to where his slaves were sitting to have a look at his new possessions. He stood in front of Tom, who was dressed in his best suit, a white cotton shirt and large leather boots. "Get up!" he shouted. Tom stood up as well as he could with chains on his hands and feet. Legree pulled Tom by the chain around his neck to the part of the boat where Tom's trunk stood. He opened it and found the pair of dirty old trousers and the old coat that Tom wore when he cleaned out the St. Clare *stables*. "Put these on and take those boots off!" he ordered. As he changed his clothes, Tom took his Bible out of his good trouser pocket and put it in the old ones. Legree picked up the good trousers and began taking things out of the pockets and throwing them overboard. He found a hymn book and held it up.

"Christian, are you?" he asked Tom.

"Yes, sir," Tom replied.

"Well, I'll soon have that out of you. I've got no time at my place for niggers who sit around singing and praying all day. I'm your church now. Do you understand, nigger?" he shouted.

But Tom did not answer. He just looked down with a heavy heart. Legree walked back to Tom's trunk, picked it up and took it over to where the deck hands were standing. One by one, Legree took Tom's best clothes out of the trunk and sold them. When he had finished that, he picked up the empty trunk and sold it to the highest bidders. The slaves continued to sit in

stable, a place where you keep horses

silence as the white men laughed at Legree's "sale" of Tom's only possessions.

"There. You won't be needing those any more, boy!" he shouted to Tom. "One suit and one pair of shoes is all you're going to use for the next year."

Legree then walked over to the young girl and put his hand under her chin to lift her face. He saw the look of fear in her eyes.

"When you look at me, girl, you smile, do you hear?" he told her. "I don't want to see that look in your eye again, understand?" He then looked around at all the others and held his *fist* up before them.

"Do you see this?" he asked looking around at the men. "This hand is so hard because I've used it *knocking* niggers down." He turned to Tom and looked him in the eye. He held his fist so close to Tom's face that Tom moved his head away quickly. "I haven't met a nigger yet I couldn't knock down with one blow!" he shouted. "So do what I tell you because I show no mercy."

The other passengers on the boat watched the whole performance but nobody spoke against Legree. There were some who were against Legree and other plantation owners like him but were not prepared to say so in public. There were others on the boat who thought that Legree's manner was the only right one to have with black slaves. The boat continued its voyage up the muddy Red River until it stopped several hours later at a small town where Legree and his slaves, and many of the other passengers, went ashore.

fist, a closed hand
knock, to hit

Dark Places

From the small town Legree took his slaves in a wagon to their new home. The road to the plantation seemed like the road to death. The country on each side was flat and very few plants grew there. The earth was red and there were large areas of *swamp* where snakes could be seen sliding in the grass. The slaves who were chained in the back of the cart grew sadder and sadder as the hours went by and the land around them grew uglier.

Legree kept himself entertained by drinking whisky as he drove the horses forwards. He was the only one in good spirits. At one point, he turned around and looked at the silent faces behind him.

"You!" he shouted. "Come on, sing!" Tom began to sing one of his favourite hymns about suffering and going home. "Stop that! Stop! I didn't ask for any of that, did I? Sing something happy. Quick!"

One of the other men started to sing a simple nonsense song. The others joined in, but without feeling. Only Legree seemed to enjoy their singing. He turned and smiled at the young girl, Emmeline, who sat behind him, and put his hand on her *trembling* shoulder.

"If you're a good girl, I'm going to give you some earrings when we get home," he told her. "And you won't have to work hard out in the fields. I'll look after you and you'll live like a real lady. Why are you so afraid? You'll be all right. Only be a good girl."

The house was even more depressing than the road.

swamp, an area of land near a lake or river that is always wet
tremble, a feeling you have when you are cold or afraid

It was once the house of a very rich man who had built beautiful gardens around it. After his death Legree had bought it. Now there were no gardens, no flowers, everything was *neglected*. Many of the windows were broken and *shutters* were hanging by one *hinge*. When the cart got to the house the slaves were pushed by two cruel-looking black men - Legree's foremen - towards some little dirty wooden huts quite far from the house. Inside there was only dirty *straw*. One of these little huts, which would be better for pigs than human beings, was going to be Tom's new home. This was not what Tom had hoped for when he left Orleans. He thought at least he would have a place to hang his clothes and a shelf for his Bible when his work was done. But here there was not one piece of furniture, not even a bed.

"Which one's mine?" he asked one of the foremen.

"It doesn't matter. They're all the same. They've all got three or four other niggers in them. Just take any one."

The other slaves did not come back until an hour after sundown. Tom watched them as they walked slowly back from the fields towards their huts, hungry, exhausted and hopeless. He knew that one or two of them would die in a month or less. Even the thought of eating did not make them happy. There was no meal ready for them. Each slave was given flour with which they could make dry bread on a fire and very little else. Tom watched the other slaves making their bread and

neglected, not cared for
shutter, a wooden cover on the outside of a window
hinge, a metal device on which windows and doors turn
straw, dried yellow stems of crops - used as bedding or food for animals

helped two of the women who were so tired that they had hardly any strength left after their day under the hot southern sun. This was the first kindness anyone had shown them in months. One of them saw Tom had a book.

"What's that you've got there? It looks like a Bible," she said. "I haven't seen a Bible since I was in Kentucky."

"It is a Bible. Are you from Kentucky, too?" Tom asked.

"Many years ago," she answered. "we all used to sit down and listen to the Missis reading us stories from it but that was a long time ago now. Here we only hear shouting and whipping."

"Come to me," Tom read from the Bible, "All you who work in the fields and are weak. I'll give you rest."

"Good words!" said the woman. "Who said them?"

"God did," said Tom.

"Well, I wish I could find him," said the woman. "I don't think I'll ever find rest again. My body hurts all over and when I go to sleep it seems like only a couple of hours before one of the foremen is shouting at me to wake up and start work again. If I knew where that man God was, I'd go and find him."

"God is here," Tom smiled. "God is everywhere."

"How can you say such a thing?" the woman continued. "Anyway, I can't sit here talking. I need some sleep."

Tom sat by the fire trying to read his Bible as the other slaves went to their straw beds to sleep. He looked up to the clear night sky and said to himself, "Is God here?" It was a little hard to believe. He walked over to his hut and found an empty place in the dirty straw. The other slaves were already asleep. Tom, too, fell asleep very quickly and in his dreams he saw a little girl smiling at him. It was Eva reading from the Bible. She was reading a passage about hope.

The Cotton Fields

Working in the fields one day, Tom found himself next to a new-comer; a woman who did not look like a slave. She was tall and slim, with delicate hands and feet. She looked intelligent and she moved elegantly. She must have been between thirty-five and forty years old, and looked as though she had had a very wild and romantic history. She had once been very beautiful but the lines on her face were from pain and suffering. Tom did not know who she was or where she came from. But she was known to the other slaves. They said hateful things to her as she walked past but she took no notice of them and continued working in silence.

On the other side of Tom was another woman. She was very ill, and was so weak she could hardly work. Tom took several handfuls of cotton from his bag and put it into hers to help her.

"No, don't, don't!" she cried. "You'll get into trouble."

Just then Sambo, one of the foremen, came up and kicked her to the ground. "Get on with your work, woman!" He swung his whip and hit Tom across the face. The woman was so weak she could not get up. "Oh, God. I wish I was dead," Tom heard her say. When the foreman left, Tom put all the cotton he had in the sick woman's bag.

“You mustn’t do that,” said the other woman, whose name was Cassy. “When you’ve been here a month, you’ll stop helping other people. It’s hard enough to take care of your own skin.” And she put some of her own cotton into Tom’s empty bag.

At the end of the day the slaves had to take all the cotton they had collected to a big room where it was weighed. Legree was there talking to the foremen. One of them told his master that Tom had put cotton in the sick woman’s bag. Legree was pleased to hear about it. Since the day on the boat Legree had decided he was going to be hard on Tom. He didn’t want people on the farm taking an interest in Christianity and thinking about things. He wanted to make sure that Tom knew who was in charge. “Miss Cassy helped to fill the woman’s basket, too, sir,” said another foreman.

“So Cassy’s been working hard, has she?” asked Legree seriously.

“She picks like she’s got the devil in her fingers,” the foreman replied.

“I believe she has, too,” said Legree quietly and spat on the floor.

The slaves stood in a line and Legree wrote down the weights of each bag of cotton. Tom had easily enough cotton but waited to make sure the sick woman was also all right. But when she walked towards Legree, trying to carry her heavy bag of cotton, Legree did not even weigh it.

“Too light again!” he shouted. “Stand over here. I’m going to show you what I think of people who don’t do their work. As the woman walked over to one side of the room, the other woman, Cassy, came up to weigh her cotton. Legree smiled and said something to her in

French. But Cassy did not smile. She looked at Legree with hate in her eyes and said something back to him between her teeth, also in French, and the others could not understand it. Legree raised his fist but the woman did not move. Tom saw that Cassy had some kind of power over Legree, who now walked away towards where Tom was standing.

"Tom," he said in an almost friendly voice. "You know I didn't buy you just to work as a cotton-picker. I want you to be a foreman, too. And you can start right now. I want you to take that woman outside and whip her," he said, pointing at the sick woman.

"I'm sorry Mas'r, but I can't do that," Tom said. "I've never done that before and I never will. It's not possible."

"I'll show you what's possible!" shouted Legree and hit Tom again and again in the face. When Tom fell to the floor, Legree stopped. "There. Now will you say you can't do it?"

"Yes, sir, Mas'r," said Tom, lifting his hand to clean the blood from his nose and mouth. "I'll work all day and all night, too, if you want me to, but I'll never do this thing because it isn't right. I'll never do it - never!" Tom spoke very quietly and the other slaves were afraid of what Legree would do next.

At first he was so surprised that he did not know what to say. Then he shouted, "I don't care what a dirty nigger thinks. You do what I tell you to do. Isn't that what it says in your Bible, that you should *obey* your master? Well, I paid twelve hundred dollars for you, so

obey, to do what you are told

you're mine, you hear, body and soul." He gave Tom a kick in the stomach with his big boot.

"No, sir, Mas'r," said Tom. "My soul isn't yours. It's mine. Nobody can buy or sell it. You can do what you like to me, but my soul's mine, and you can't take it away."

"Well, let's see what I can and can't do, shall we? Boys, take him outside and give him a whipping!"

Tom was dragged outside by the two foremen. The other slaves watched in silent fear.

Miss Cassy

After being whipped, Tom was left outside, lying in the middle of cotton bags and broken farm machines. His body was covered with blood and he could not even move. The air around him was full of *mosquitoes* that bit him all the time but he did not have the strength to cover himself. The worst thing was not the mosquitoes, though. The only thing he could think about was water.

"Oh, God, take me, please," he prayed as he lay there.

Then he heard footsteps and saw someone walking towards him with a lamp. "Oh, water, give me some water please, for mercy's sake," he said weakly. It was Cassy. She gave him water from a large bottle.

"Drink all you want," she said. "This isn't the first time I've had to do this, giving people water after a whipping."

mosquito, flying insect that bites and sucks blood

"Thank you, Missis," said Tom, when the bottle was empty.

"Don't call me Missis," she said. "Can't you see I'm a miserable slave like you?" She took some wet cloths and put them onto Tom's broken skin. He felt much better for their cooling effect on his burning body.

"It's no use doing what you did today. Legree will always win, don't you see?" she said sitting on the floor next to him. "You must give up."

"Good Lord, I can never give up," he said. "How can I?"

"Lord?" she asked. "There's no Lord here. I've been here for five years and this place is hell on earth. There's no law here. You can die and be eaten by the dogs and nobody'll care. He always gets what he wants. Look at me. Can you believe I've lived with that man in the same house for five years? I come from a good family and got an education. Do you think I wanted to live with him? I hate him but there's nothing I can do about it. Now he's got this new fifteen-year-old girl and he wants to live with her now. She brought her Bible, too. Ha!" She laughed with a cruel, hard smile.

"Oh, Jesus, Jesus, help, save us," said Tom between his tears.

"Why do you want to help these miserable dogs, anyway?" the woman continued. "They wouldn't help you if you were in need. They are just as cruel as Legree and all the others."

"They're just poor people, Missis. What made them cruel? I'll never give up. If I did, I'd get just like them. I've lost everything I ever had - my wife, my children, my home, a kind master who was going to give me my freedom if he'd lived another week. I can't lose heaven, too, Missis. It's the only thing I've got. I'm not going to get *wicked* as well."

There was a long silence as they both sat there thinking. Then Tom remembered where they had thrown his coat. "Missis, could you go over there and get my coat for me? It's behind that machine there."

She came back with his coat and he took the Bible from the pocket. He opened it and found a page that had been read many times before. "Could you just read this to me, Missis? It helps me better than water."

Cassy read him the story of Jesus's walk to Calvary where he was left to die on the cross. She read the story with some interest and then cried when she came to the part that said, "Forgive them, Father, for they know not what they do."

"You see, Missis. He did it. They *stoned* him in the streets but he never stopped. He knew what he was doing was right so he carried on. We must never give up. We must always believe in what is right and hold on to it."

"But it's so hard," Cassy said looking into Tom's eyes. "You can't keep it going. I know because I've seen how people change. I had a very good life before and lived in a big house with a man I loved. Then I was sold because the man owed lots of money and my children were taken away. In the end I was sold to Legree and ended up here in this place. I used to go to church and read the Bible. But how can you believe in God in a place like this?"

Tom was going to say something but she stopped him and said, "No, get some sleep, if you can." She got him

wicked, bad
to stone, to punish someone by throwing stones at them

some more water and tried to make him feel a litle more comfortable. Then she got up and left him.

A Plan

Tom worked on the cotton plantation for many more months and became a good friend of Cassy. Slowly he began to talk to the other slaves and many began to find hope in his example and from the stories he told them from his book. Legree hated him more than ever and Tom was very often beaten by Legree or his foremen, but never so hard that he could not work again the next day. Legree needed as many workers as he could get.

The Bible was the only pleasure Tom had in life. Everything around him was sad. He began to see that there was not even any more hope. His wife and family did not know where he was and he would never be able to write to them. He knew that Ophelia had written a letter to Kentucky to explain what had happened to him in Orleans. But Legree would never post a letter from him in the town or give him a letter if he ever received one. The only thing left to him was his Bible and his belief in God.

Tom saw how, once or twice, a slave tried to escape, but it was impossible. There was nowhere to go. The plantation was in the middle of nowhere and surrounded by marshes. The other plantation owners would kill you if they saw you escaping. Legree and the other owners enjoyed hunting for a runaway slave. They sent their savage dogs after them and often found the slave was already half-dead before they took the dogs away. Legree once carried a dead slave back to the farm from the marshes and left him hanging outside to show the others what would happen to them if they tried to escape. The nearest town was days away on foot and a runaway slave would probably never get that far before he was shot dead. Tom knew that he would probably die here but he almost welcomed the idea.

In fact Tom was not at all sad. He enjoyed seeing how his words helped to change the other slaves. They became less cruel and he could see there was new hope in their eyes.

Cassy slowly changed, too. She became friendly to the other girl that Legree had bought at the market. The girl looked on Cassy as a kind of aunt. Cassy tried as hard as she could to protect the girl from Legree, knowing from her own experience that it was better to have as little to do with the man as possible. Legree was afraid of Cassy. She was the only person on the plantation who could stand up to him and sometimes tell him what to do. The day she worked in the fields with Tom was the result of an argument between her and Legree about the arrival of the young girl. Because she was so wild, Legree never knew what she would do next. This was what made him afraid of her.

Because Cassy kept the girl Emmeline away from Legree, he began to drink a lot. Most nights he would fall asleep in a chair, surrounded by his dogs and completely drunk. Emmeline and Cassy slept in the same room but the girl was always afraid of Legree coming into her room in the middle of the night.

"Oh, why can't we leave this place? Couldn't we run into the swamps or somewhere? It would be better to be dead out there with the snakes than stay here with him!" she once told Cassy.

"There's nowhere to go, child," Cassy replied. "And if you do run away and they catch you, it'll be worse. It's better to stay here and do what he tells you. That's what I did and it's the only way."

But Cassy had a plan. There was a room at the top of the house that was always locked and full of furniture. Legree never went there and nor did anybody else. There was a story that a ghost of a dead woman was in the room. When Legree was not in the house, Cassy began to move some of the furniture out of this room and into the others to make some space. She often wore a white sheet over her head and would go up into the room at night. Stories began to go around the farm that a female ghost had been seen walking around the house. These stories made Legree more nervous than most other people would be. For some reason he had a *fascination* for the *supernatural*. He began to have nightmares about ghosts, and drank more whisky and brandy to help him sleep.

One night when he was lying on the floor, drunk, Cassy woke Emmeline and took her up to the locked room at the top of the house, locking themselves inside. When Legree woke early next morning he found the two women were gone. He quickly ordered the foremen to organize a hunt with the slaves and dogs to find them in the marshes. Most were happy to do this instead of their boring job of picking cotton. Tom was one of the few slaves who would not help and stayed where he was. Cassy and Emmeline could see the confusion as Legree organized the hunt from the

fascination, a special interest
supernatural, something which can not be explained by science

room's window. Cassy had taken enough food and water as well as clothes and other things so that the women would have something to do. They stayed in the room all day, keeping as quiet as they could until the hunt came back in the evening.

Legree was extremely angry and thought that Tom must know where the escaped slaves were as he seemed quite happy and had not wanted to go with the hunt.

"If I find out you know where they are, Tom, I've decided I'm going to kill you," he told him.

"Yes, Mas'r," Tom replied and looked at the floor.

"So are you going to tell me where they are, nigger?"

"I can't help you, sir."

The next morning while it was still dark, the hunt got ready for the next search. Legree had asked for help from the other plantation owners and they were all sitting on their horses outside the house drinking brandy.

"Look, Emmeline, they're going out again today," Cassy said, waking the girl. The hunt moved away in different directions and there were hardly any slaves left on the farm. Dressed in their white sheets, Cassy and Emmeline ran down the stairs, out of the front door and towards the main road some miles away.

The Hero

Legree was so angry about the escape of his two women, that he turned all his rage against Tom. Tom knew where the women had gone and how they had escaped but was not going to tell anyone.

"I'm giving you one last chance, Tom, to save yourself!" Legree shouted. "Now where did those women go?"

"Mas'r, I'd do anything you wanted me to. I'd give you the last drop of blood in my heart if you were dying and I could save you, that's the truth. But I'm not going to tell you. You can do what you want to me."

These words seemed to stop Legree for a second. But it was only a second. In front of all the other slaves he gave Tom the biggest beating he had ever given any man. Tom did not once try to defend himself. He was hit by punches and whips and the life was kicked out of him as he lay on the floor. As the last kick came against his head, Tom slowly opened his eyes and looked up to his master standing over him.

"You poor, poor man. There's nothing more you can do to me. I forgive you with all my soul!" he said and then closed his eyes again.

Tom's words had a tremendous effect on the hearts of those present. The black slaves who had watched his beating saw the goodness of the man and the depth of his suffering. Even the cruel foremen looked at each other and said, "That was a terrible thing we did today!" One of them tried to get some brandy to try and put some life back into Tom.

"I'm sorry, Tom," he said holding the glass to the man's face. "We've been so bad to you."

"I forgive you," said Tom. "And Jesus will forgive you, too, if you ask him."

Tom closed his eyes again and everyone there, including the foremen, cried at the goodness of the man and the evil he had fought against.

A Young Visitor

Two days later a young man arrived at the house with a horse and cart. It was the young George Shelby. The Shelby family had received Ophelia's letter which told of Tom's sale to Legree at the Orleans slave market. Since Tom had last heard from them, Mr Shelby had been very ill and had finally died. Mrs Shelby was so sad after the death of her husband that it was her son, now a young man, who began to take control of the farm. It was a long time before Mrs Shelby could fully understand all the business deals Mr Shelby had had when he was alive. Finally, they organized the family money and George was sent down to Orleans to find out where Tom had gone and to buy him back.

"What can I do for you, stranger?" Legree asked when George Shelby arrived at his door.

"I'm looking for a black slave called Tom. I want to buy him back."

"Yes, I bought him and it was the worst money I ever spent. Made me lose two slaves, he did, and he still won't tell me where they went even after the biggest beating I ever gave a man."

"Where is he now?" George asked.

"He's over there, dying in that shed," a little slave boy who was holding the horse told him. Legree kicked the boy and shouted at him but George walked straight over to the shed. He found Tom lying on the floor and not moving. He couldn't move because all the nerves in his body were destroyed. He was only alive now because the slaves had brought him water and some of their own food to feed him.

"Oh, dear Uncle Tom! Speak to me. It's George, Mas'r George. Don't you know me?"

"Mas'r George?" said Tom's weak voice as his eyes opened very slowly. He seemed confused. "Mas'r George!" Slowly his face changed and a smile came into the eyes of the dying man. "I knew they wouldn't forget me. Thank you, Lord! Now I can die a happy man!"

"You can't die Tom, I'm taking you home."

"It's too late Mas'r George. A new master has bought

my soul and he's going to take me with him. Heaven is even better than Kentucky." Tom took George's hand. "You mustn't tell Chloe you found me like this. Tell her the Lord's always been with me, making life easy, and that I've always loved her and the children. Give my love to Mas'r and Missis Shelby. Mas'r George, what a wonderful thing it is to be a Christian!"

Tom smiled for one last time and then George felt all the strength leave Tom's hand. Old Uncle Tom was dead.

At that moment, Legree walked in.

"Well, you've had all you could take from him," said George. "How much do you want for him."

"Nothing. He's only a dead nigger. You can bury him where you like."

This man made George so angry that he turned without thinking and punched Legree straight on the nose, knocking him to the floor. Two slaves helped him carry the dead body of Tom to the cart.

"Please, Mas'r. I'll be a good slave," said one of them. "Please buy me, Mas'r, please!"

"I'm afraid I can't, sorry," George replied. Then he said to himself, "I'm going to do everything I can to stop this cruelty for the rest of my days."

Reunion

Cassy and Emmeline had run two or three miles from the house and then changed into some very elegant clothes which they had brought with them. People were looking for a pair of badly dressed slaves, not very elegantly dressed ladies with dark skin. The plan worked. After a few hours, the ladies were in the town and waiting for the next river boat. Cassy had lived an elegant life before arriving at Legree's so nobody in the town found it strange that the two women were travelling together. On the boat, they both stayed in their cabin so as not to attract any attention. When they got to the Mississippi River they had to change boats.

George was on the same boat and also planned to take the boat up the Mississippi towards Kentucky. On this boat it was safer for the two women to show their faces and they began to eat at the dining tables with the others. George watched Cassy and had a strange feeling that he recognised her from somewhere. She could see him watching her and it made her nervous. She told him everything about their escape and hoped he would not send them back. But George was, of course, very happy to hear of someone escaping from Legree's plantation and she stopped worrying about him.

One day on the boat, a French woman began to ask him questions about Kentucky. She knew some of the same people that he knew so she must have lived there once.

"Do you know the Harris family?" she asked him.

"Yes, very well. They live near me."

"Did you ever know a mulatto slave they bought called George?"

"George Harris? Yes, of course. But I haven't seen him for many years. He married one of our women and they escaped to Canada," he replied.

"Escaped? That's wonderful!" the woman smiled.

"Do you know him?"

"Yes, he's my brother!" the woman said. "George Harris is my brother. I was sold down South when he was a boy and I've never seen him since. I knew he had been sold to a Mr Harris in Kentucky and, now that my husband has died and left me some money, I planned to go to Kentucky and buy his freedom."

"He told me he had a sister called Emily," George said.

"That's me, I'm Emily de Thoux," she smiled. "Tell me, what kind of a man is he?"

"A very fine man. He was very intelligent even though he was forced to be a slave. His wife is a very beautiful girl. She could read and write and was good at sewing. She was very religious, too, and a good singer."

"Was she born in your house?" the woman asked.

"No. My father bought her when she was eight in New Orleans. He paid a lot of money for her then because she was so beautiful."

Cassy was listening to this conversation from the next table with great interest.

"You don't know the name of the people he bought her from, do you?" she asked.

"Yes, they were quite a rich family down there who then had some money problems and sold a mother and her child. The mother was already sold. I think their name was Simmons, if I remember correctly."

"Oh, my God!" said Cassy, and fell to the floor in a faint. When she came round again, she could not believe what George had told her. Could it be true? Was she really going to see her daughter Eliza again?

The conversations continued until they reached Kentucky, and George was sure from what Cassy told him that Eliza was her daughter. He signed the papers which gave Eliza her freedom and Cassy took them with her. She and Emily de Thoux continued their journey together up to Canada. After a few weeks asking around at the escaped slave centres, they found out where George and Eliza lived.

The young family were enjoying a good life in Canada. George had a good job and Eliza had given birth to a baby daughter. Their son Harry was doing very well at school and was beginning to look just like his father. When Emily and Cassy walked into their house in Montreal, all their lives changed forever. Emily had married a rich man and had enough money to share with her brother and his family. They all decided to go to France where George got himself a university education.

Emmeline fell in love with a man she met on the boat and they later married.

Chloe's Sadness

When Mrs Shelby heard that her son was returning from Orleans, everybody was excited, especially Chloe, who had taken time free off work to be at the Shelbys' when her husband arrived.

"What did Mas'r George say in his letter, Missis?" Chloe asked.

"He just wrote one line, Chloe. He just said when he was coming home."

Mrs Shelby was very nervous about her son's arrival. He was normally a good writer and it was unusual for him to write only a short note like this one. She knew something was wrong. Then they heard wheels approaching the farm.

"There they are!" shouted Chloe, and ran over to the front door of the house. Mrs Shelby ran to put her arms around her son while Chloe looked over their shoulders towards the empty cart. George quickly walked over to where Chloe stood and took her hand in his.

"Oh, poor Chloe, I'm sorry!" he cried. "It was too late. I'd have paid anything to get him back but he's gone to a better place."

They walked back into the house. Mrs Shelby cried but Chloe made no sound. She just stood with her eyes wide open looking through the window.

"I knew it. I knew they'd murder him on one of those southern plantations." She began to walk towards the door but Mrs Shelby sat her down in a chair and Chloe's eyes filled with tears.

About a month later George called all the servants together. He had something to say to them. He was carrying a pile of papers, certificates which gave every one of them their freedom. He called their names and gave each one their certificate. Not all of them, though, were happy.

"Please don't send us away Mas'r George. We're happy just being here. You can have the papers back, we don't want them."

"Good friends," George told them all. "Nobody has to leave. There is still the same work as there was before and we still need everybody here. But now you are free men and women. You'll get paid for your work. The main thing is that if anything happens to me, you can't be sold. I hope to teach you how to use your new rights to freedom. I hope you'll be happy to learn. But now you are free. So let us all thank God for the blessing of freedom."

An old black man started a prayer of thanksgiving to God, which the others joined in with. When it was over, George spoke again.

"I'm sure you all remember old Uncle Tom. He asked me to say goodbye to you all. It is because of Tom that I decided never to have another slave while it was possible to free him, that nobody should be taken away from their family and friends and left to die on a plantation. So remember, every time you *rejoice* in your new freedom, that it is Uncle Tom and his family you should thank. When you see Uncle Tom's cabin remember to follow in his footsteps and be as good and honest Christians as he was."

rejoice, to be glad

QUESTIONS AND ACTIVITIES

Questions

1. What was it that Mr Shelby did not like about Haley?
2. Why did Shelby feel he needed to sell Tom?
3. Why do you think he waited before telling his wife?
4. Why did George's owner take him out of the factory and back to the farm?
5. What made George decide to escape to Canada?
6. Why did he choose Canada?
7. In what way was Uncle Tom a religious leader on the farm?

Language Activity

There are many differences between American English and the English spoken in Britain. For example, people who work on farms in America are called "farm hands". In Britain, people would say "farm labourers". Below is a list of common American words and their British equivalents. Try to match the words - use a dictionary to help you if necessary.

American:

elevator	closet	freeway	eraser	yard
cookies	candy	sidewalk	vacation	the fall
truck	garbage	gasoline	apartment	subway

British

garden	flat	pavement	autumn	biscuits
lorry	petrol	holiday	sweets	rubber
wardrobe	rubbish	lift	motorway	underground
railway				

Questions

1. How did Mrs Shelby react to her husband's decision to sell Tom and Harry?
2. Why did Tom not run away with Eliza?
3. What did the farm hands do to stop Haley chasing Eliza and Harry?
4. How did Mrs Shelby feel about this?
5. Why did people not stop Eliza to ask why she was walking on the road?
6. Why was it so important for black people to get to Ohio?

General Knowledge Activity

Uncle Tom's Cabin was written in 1852. Between 1861 and 1865 there was a war between the southern states and the northern states in America. Among other things the southern states wanted to keep the system of slavery and the north wanted to stop it. Which of the following states fought to keep slavery?

Iowa	Georgia	Mississippi	Florida	New York
California	Alaska	Alabama	South Carolina	
Oregon	Texas	Virginia	Illinois	Nebraska

Questions

1. What did Mrs Shelby promise Tom?
2. Why was the man who helped Eliza out of the river breaking his country's laws?
3. How did Haley's luck change after Eliza escaped?
4. What was the deal between Haley and Marks and Loker?
5. What sad event had happened to both Eliza and Mrs Bird?

Activity

This summary of the chapter "A politician with human feelings" contains a number of mistakes. Rewrite the summary as it should be.

Eliza swam across the Ohio River through the ice carrying little Harry on her back. She was helped out of the river by a politician called Mr Symmes, who was a neighbour of Mr Shelby. Eliza went to the house of Mr and Mrs Bird. Mr Bird was president of Kentucky and had come home for a rest. Mr and Mrs Bird thought that people should never help runaway slaves and when they found Eliza in their garden their first thought was to take her to the local sheriff. After they heard Eliza's story of her escape from Shelby's house in Mississippi, they decided to wait for Haley to come the next day and give Eliza and her son back to him.

Questions

True or False?

1. Chloe knew that Tom would never come back from the South.
2. Tom wondered if there really was a God.
3. Mrs Shelby did not want to see Tom and Chloe.
4. Haley was friendly to Tom when he saw him.
5. Haley chained Tom up so that he would not escape.
6. Mas'r George cried when he saw Tom leave.
7. Mas'r George gave Tom a silver dollar.

Understanding the text

Put the following sentences in the correct order as they happened in the story.

Lucy's baby was sold
Tom saved Eva's life
Haley bought some more slaves at the market in Kentucky
Augustine St. Clare bought Tom
Lucy killed herself
Tom got on a river-boat to Orleans
Lucy looked for her husband at Louisville

Vocabulary building

Below is a list of words we use to describe people's personality. Which of them could you use to describe these characters?

Tom	Ophelia	Marie St. Clare	Mrs Bird
Augustine St. Clare	Haley	George	Eliza

Personality adjectives:

idealistic	serious	cruel	determined
selfish	brave	aggressive	generous
intelligent	dishonest	hard-working	
lazy	gentle	practical	

Are there any other words you can think of to describe these characters?

Questions

1. What are the main differences between Augustine St. Clare, Marie St. Clare and Ophelia in a) their relationship to the servants and b) their feelings about slavery?
2. What did St. Clare say about the situation of black people in the northern states? Did he think it was better or worse than that of slaves in the South?
3. George said he would fight to the last breath to defend himself and his family. How did this compare with Tom's attitude?
4. Why do you think that Eva was not sad as she lay on her death-bed?
5. How did Legree's house compare with that of St. Clare?
6. The writer called Tom's death a victory. What did she mean by this?

Discussion activity

Which of these statements do you think the writer would agree with? Give reasons to justify your opinion.

1. Slavery is acceptable if the slave owners are not cruel to their servants.
2. Everybody should be treated with the same respect, regardless of their skin colour.
3. Life is easier and better if you believe in God.
4. Violence is necessary to defend your family against others.
5. People in the northern states treated black people better than people in the South did.
6. Men are more intelligent than women.
7. Women are more caring and less violent than men.
8. People should never break the law.

Notes:

Notes:

Notes:

Notes:

Notes:

Notes:

Notes: